Lesson Plan 1

NeoPopRealism Ink Pen/ Pattern Drawing - NeoWhimsy Goldfish:
[Carassius auratus auratus]

Grades 6-8, adapt.3-5, 9-12
Duration: three 45 minute class periods
Media Type: Ink & Pen Drawing
Subject Integration: Science

OBJECTIVES:
Students will create their own ink pen/ pattern drawings after studying NeoPopRealism ink pen/ pattern drawing style and the drawings by NeoPopRealism creator Nadia Russ.

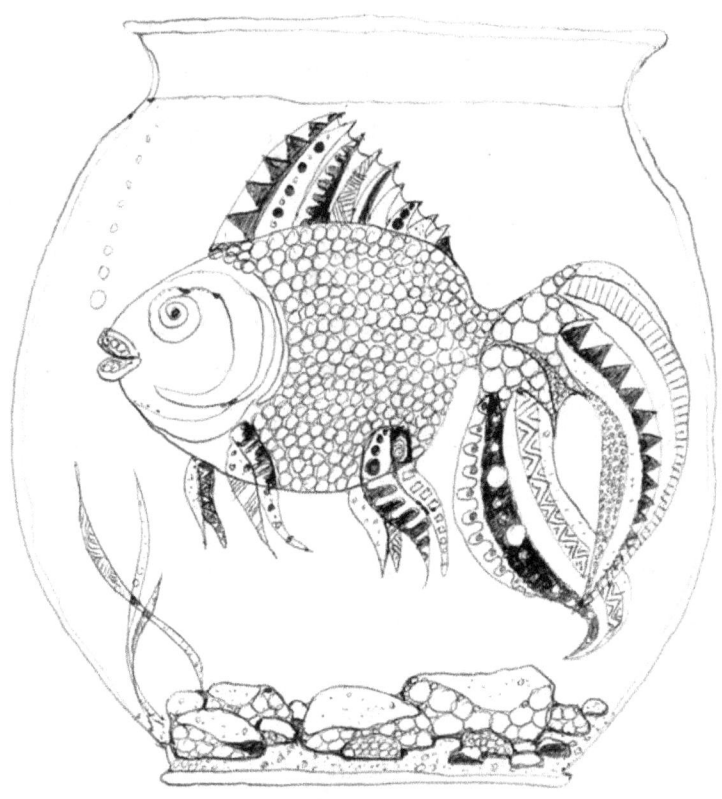

The Goldfish

ASSESSMENT:
Students will demonstrate an understanding of NeoPopRealism ink pen/ pattern drawing technique inspired by Nadia Russ' drawings (see posters' links in Resources below), incorporating a variety of patterns into a drawing.

MATERIALS:
White paper 8.5"x 11"
Ink pen 0.7mm

PROCEDURES:
Day 1:
Display on the wall posters with images of Nadia Russ' ink pen/ pattern drawings.
Give introduction to NeoPopRealism/ NeoWhhimsies ink pen/ pattern drawing. Show Movie (2:00min) NeoPopRealism introduction:
http://goanimate.com/go/movie/0evkSruBpt7I?utm_source=emailshare&uid=/
Talk about Nadia Russ' (biography), NeoPopRealism and NeoWhimsies, the simplified NeoPopRealism ink pen pattern images (see http://neopoprealismblackwhiteink.blogspot.com/).
Discussion: What do you know about drawing? Let students compare Nadia Russ' NeoPopRealism ink pen pattern drawings and drawings by Leonardo da Vinci and others, discussing differences and similarities.
 Ask students to take notes while looking at drawings by artists Nadia Russ. Students write down 10 things they see/learn by looking at NeoPopRealism ink pen/ pattern drawings.

Talk about Goldfish, where she lives, about the goldfishfish's features. Demonstrate NeoPopRealism ink pen / pattern drawing technique to students: draw a line that creates goldfish's body and tail, then divide them into sections. These sections you fill with different repetitive patterns. Some sections should be left blank. Eraser never used: if a 'mistake' made the next repetitive patterns balance the whole composition and make this 'mistake' invisible. Use piece of white paper 8.5"x11" to draw 10 or more different samples of repetitive patterns - zigzag white/ black, dots, small circles, big circles, rectangular, waves, paralleled lines, white circles on black, dots mixed with circles, zigzags with triangles... Students will create their own samples of repetitive patterns. Students will later use these repetitive patterns' samples when creating their final drawing.

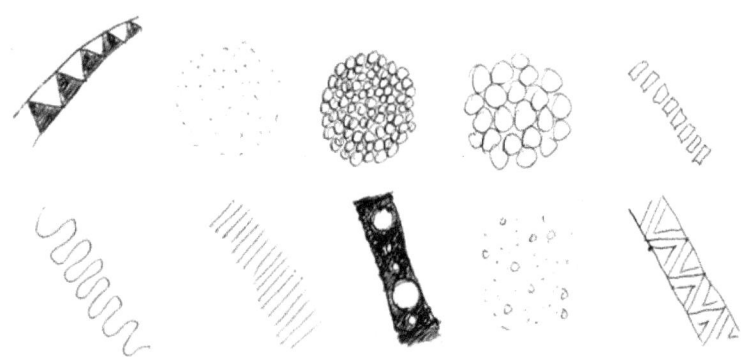

Day 2:
Students will refer to pictures of goldfish. Students will create their own fish drawings, using ink pen, including one, two or three fish in their drawing. Students will refer to ink pen/ patterns drawing samples keeping in mind when and how to use the various patterns. Students are sure to draw aquarium and include rocks, and sea grass.

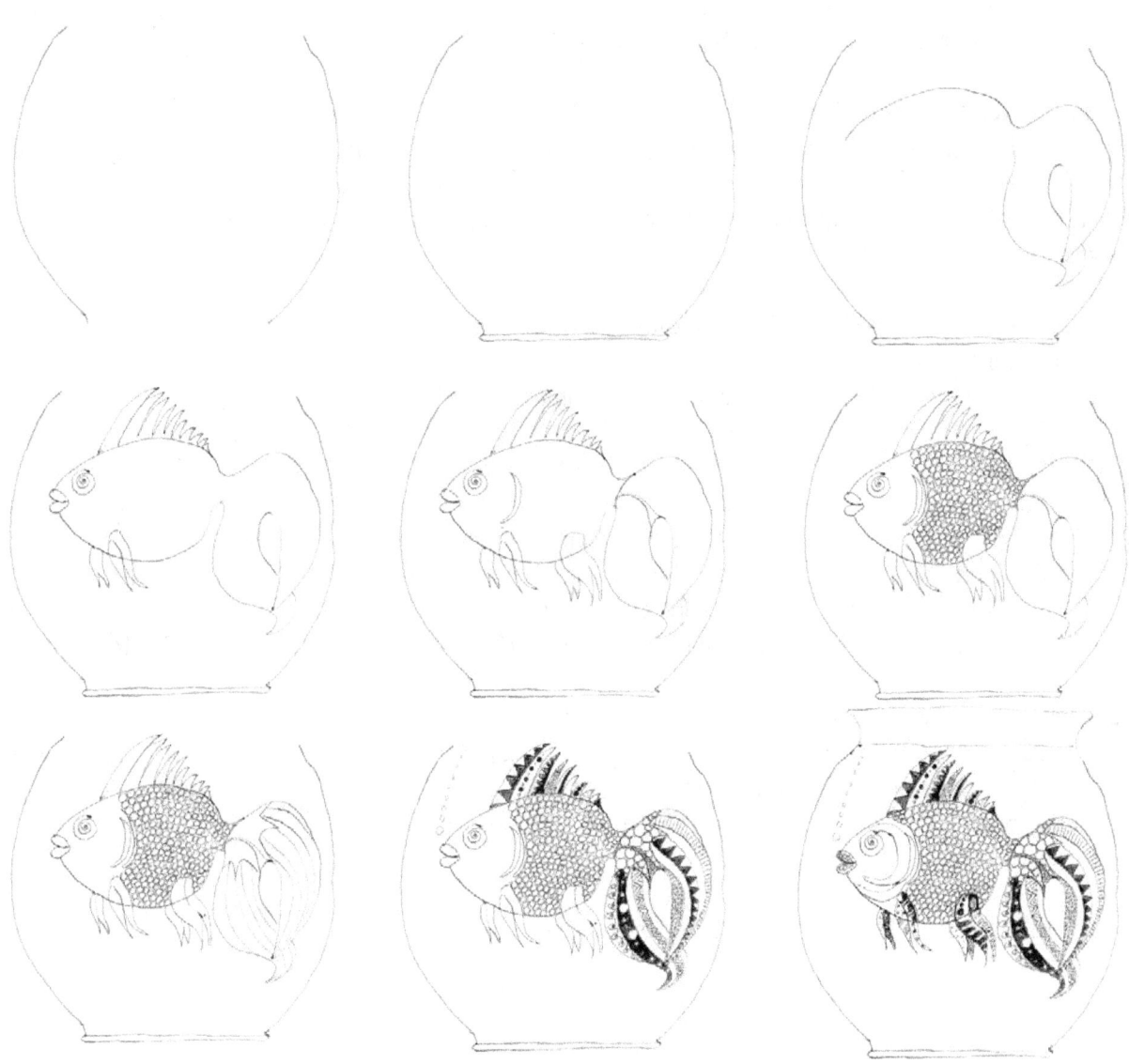

NeoPopRealisml/ NeoWhimsy ink pen pattern drawing GOLDFISH

Day 3: Students finish drawing process.
Discussion Questions:
What did you learn about NeoPopRealism ink pen/ pattern drawing that you did not know before?
What did you learn about Nadia Russ? Which repetitive pattern was your favorite? Why? What did

you find easy to accomplish within your artwork? What did you find difficult? What would you do different next time?

RESOURCES:

1. Information on NeoPopRealism ink pen/ pattern drawing, its concept and Nadia Russ biography, who created this style in 1989: see page 101 and in http://neopoprealismblackwhiteink.blogspot.com/

2. NeoPopRealism/ NeoWhimsies MOVIE #3 - introduction (2:00 min) : http://goanimate.com/go/movie/0evkSruBpt7I?utm_source=emailshare&uid=/

3. Wall decals with NeoPopRealism ink pen drawings at 33% off for educators: www.neopoprealism.net

4. Nadia Russ official website: www.nadiaruss.com
5. Photographs of goldfish.
6. Posters and/or photocopies of drawings by Leonardo da Vinci.

FOLLOW UP AND ACTIVITIES:
View Nadia Russ artwork and discuss NeoPopRealism ink pen pattern drawing style. Let each students make a question-answer 2 minutes length movie about what they have learned about NeoPopRealism/ NeoWhimsies art and Nadia Russ using website http://goanimate.com/.
Name artists-inventors and top representatives of the new styles of visual arts: Dali (Surrealism), Andy Warhol and Jasper Johns (Pop Art), Jeff Koons (Neo-Pop), Nadia Russ (NeoPopRealism).

NeoPopRealism ink pen/pattern drawing concept:
A line creates sections [often in seemed chaotic order]. Then, these sections filled with different repetitive patterns. Some sections must be left blank. Eraser never used. If a 'mistake' made, the following repetitive patterns balance the whole composition and make this 'mistake' invisible. It develops your sense of composition.

Fight bullying in school with 10 NeoPopRealism canons for happier life (see page 101 and www.nadaruss.com).

Lesson Plan 2

NeoPopRealism Abstract - Ink Pen / Pattern Drawing inspired by Nadia RUSS

Grades: adaptable all ages, including adults
Art & Music, Art & Technology

DESCRIPTION:
This lesson plan takes inspiration from Nadia RUSS art. Students will be able to define the terms "NeoPopRealism abstract" and "meditative ink pen pattern drawing", and will differentiate these from other styles and approaches.

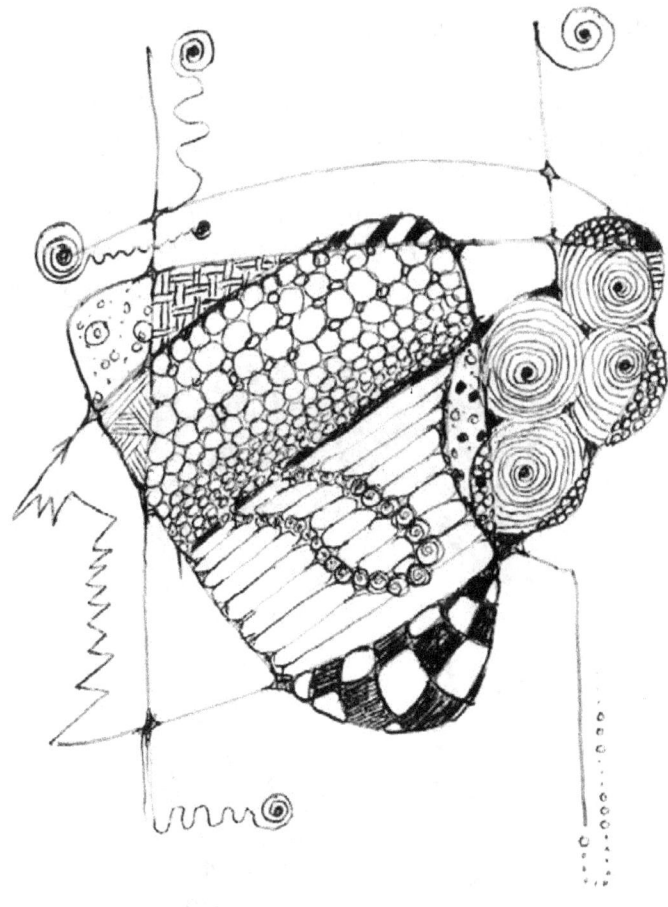

NeoPopRealist Abstract

KEYWORDS:
Nadia Russ, NeoPopRealism ink pen pattern drawing, abstract, meditative drawing.

MATERIALS:
- white paper 8.5"x11"
- Ink pen black 0.7mm
-Computer to watch a (fun) movie - an introduction to NeoPopRealism: http://goanimate.com/videos/0qwwEP0AaOew?utm_source=linkshare/

LESSON PLAN - MOTIVATION:
When you focus on success you fall into the trap of comparing yourself to others, feeling envious. Instead, focus on getting better every day, focus on excellence. Your artwork is reflection of you, your moods; also it depends on what your artistic task is.

In this lesson, you teach a fun and easy way to make authentic and original NeoPopRealism abstract drawings on a small scale. The technique is appropriate for students age six and up. It's also fun for beginners adults to learn to draw the NeoPopRealism abstracts. Display some of Nadia RUSS' posters in the classroom. Have a presentation ready to students. When drawing process begins, you can tern on music (not loud), preferably jazz.

NeoPopRealism abstract drawing is meditative. When artist draws, his/her mind is open for renewal. Nadia Russ explains NeoPopRealism abstract as the work from within, when artist expresses his/her inner world. Eraser never used because if a 'mistake' made it would disappear with the following repetitive patterns that balance the whole composition and make a 'mistake' invisible. NeoPopRealism abstract can be used as an independent piece of art and as the backgrounds for more realistic NeoPopRealism artworks (see "Mick Jagger").

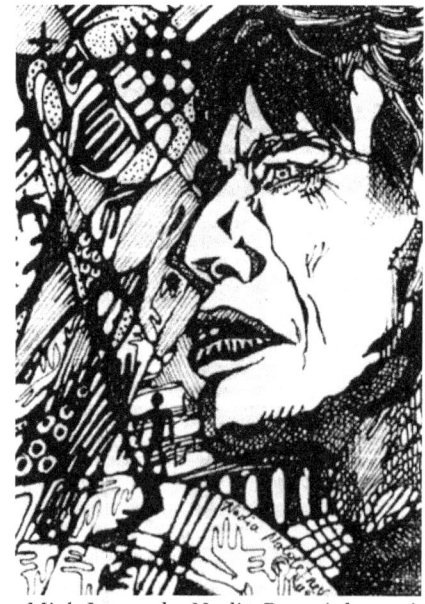

Mick Jagger by Nadia Russ, ink pen./
pattern drawing, 1994

12

NeoPopRealism

Ink & Pen Pattern Drawing

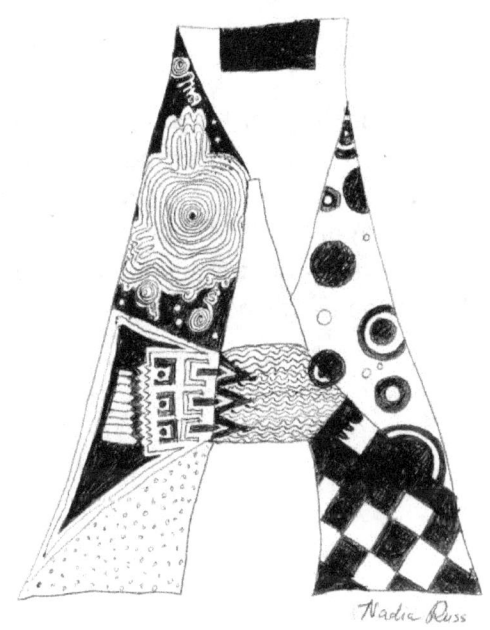

15 Most Popular
ART LESSON PLANS

adaptable to ALL GRADES

NADIA RUSS
NeoPopRealismPRESS

First time published in 2013 by NeoPopRealism PRESS
PO BOX 366
New York, NY 10013

NeoPopRealismPRESS@mail.com

NeoPopRealism Ink & Pen Pattern Drawing: 15 Most Popular ART LESSON PLANS adaptable to ALL GRADES

ISBN-13: 978-0615754659
ISBN-10: 0615754651

13 14 15 16 17   10 9 8 7 6 5 4 3 2 1

Published in the United States of America
Language: English

This book offer 15 most popular art lesson plans teaching how to draw NeoPopRealism

Author: Nadia Russ with
NeoPopRealism Press

www.neopoprealism.org

CR80

Cᴏᴎᴛᴇᴎᴛ

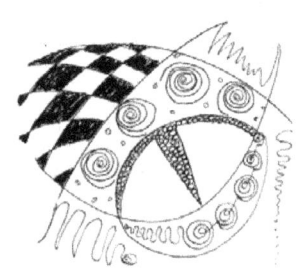

A book "NeoPopRealism Ink & Pen Pattern Drawing: 15 Most Popular Art Lesson Plans" offers the art teachers 15 lesson plans featured online. During five months, they have had 80,000 views. And now, they are available in print.

Have a wonderful journey to the world of the NeoPopRealism ink & pen pattern drawing!

LESSON PLAN - BACKGROUND AND HISTORICAL INFORMATION:
Nadia RUSS is a Ukrainian-born Russian painter/ graphic artist living in the USA, who created a style of visual arts NeoPopRealism. She is famous for innovative NeoPopRealism art and ink pen pattern drawing, including abstract, the meditative style that she created in 1989. Instead of careful copying reality - wild life or human figure, Nadia RUSS creates her artwork using imagination. As Nadia RUSS experimented and developed her distinctive techniques, her drawings became more symbolic. For her drawings she uses white paper and black ink pen. However, sometimes, she uses blue ink on white paper and gold/silver ink on black paper.

How did Nadia RUSS develop her unique and original style NeoPopRealism? RUSS had studied classical drawing and composition since she was a child, but as she studied she found herself drawn to produce less realistic, more imaginative artwork. In 1989, she created NeoPopRealism art style and ink pen pattern drawing concept: line creates sections; then, these section filled with different repetitive patterns, some section should be left blank. If artwork made on canvas using color paints and a brush, then, it would be a combination of sections filled with hot and cold color paint, partly with patterns. In 1990, RUSS exhibited her first ink pattern drawings in a group exhibition in Moscow's famous Manege. Later, she was exhibiting her artwork in the art galleries. In 1996, she moved to the Freeport, Bahamas, where her artwork gained special brightness. In 2000, she came to USA where she lives till present. Nadia Russ created a term "NeoPopRealism" January 4, 2003. Same year, she manifested her new style of visual arts NeoPopRealism internationally. In 2004, she created NeoPopRealism 10 canons for happier life. In 2006-2007, several US and European museums collected Nadia Russ' paintings and drawings and now, these artworks are in the permanent collections of these museums.

LESSON PLAN - ACTIVITY:

Hand out 8.5"x11" papers and have students write their names on the back. Let student watch the short Movie (2:00min), an introduction to NeoPopRealism:
http://goanimate.com/videos/0qwwEP0AaOew?utm_source=linkshare/

Demonstrate step-by-step how to draw the NeoPopRealist abstract image (see illustration), use ink pen Medium 0.7 mm.

Draw lines that create sections. Then, fill these sections with different patterns. Demonstrate how different types of repetitive patterns change image's character and meaning. While drawing, use imagination, it is unconscious process. This drawing is meditative.

As resources the following books can be used:
- *How to Draw NeoPopRealism Abstract Images: Ink Backgrounds*, ISBN: 978-0615527437;
- *How to Draw NeoPopRealism Advanced Abstract Images: Ink Backgrounds*, ISBN: 978-0615592558;
- *How to Draw NeoPopRealism Abstract Images: Metallic Exuberance*, ISBN: 978-0615560991;
- *Black Book for NeoPopRealism Metallic INK pen Drawing*, ISBN: 978-0615561028

Each book offers the drawing projects with visual step-by-step instructions, patterns, and pages to create the patterns' gallery. These books also contain special pages with unfinished drawings-templates that students use for training. Additionally to it these books offer information on NeoPopRealism history and its creator Nadia Russ, 10 canons for happier life, and special pages for drawing NeoPopRealism abstracts from the scratch.

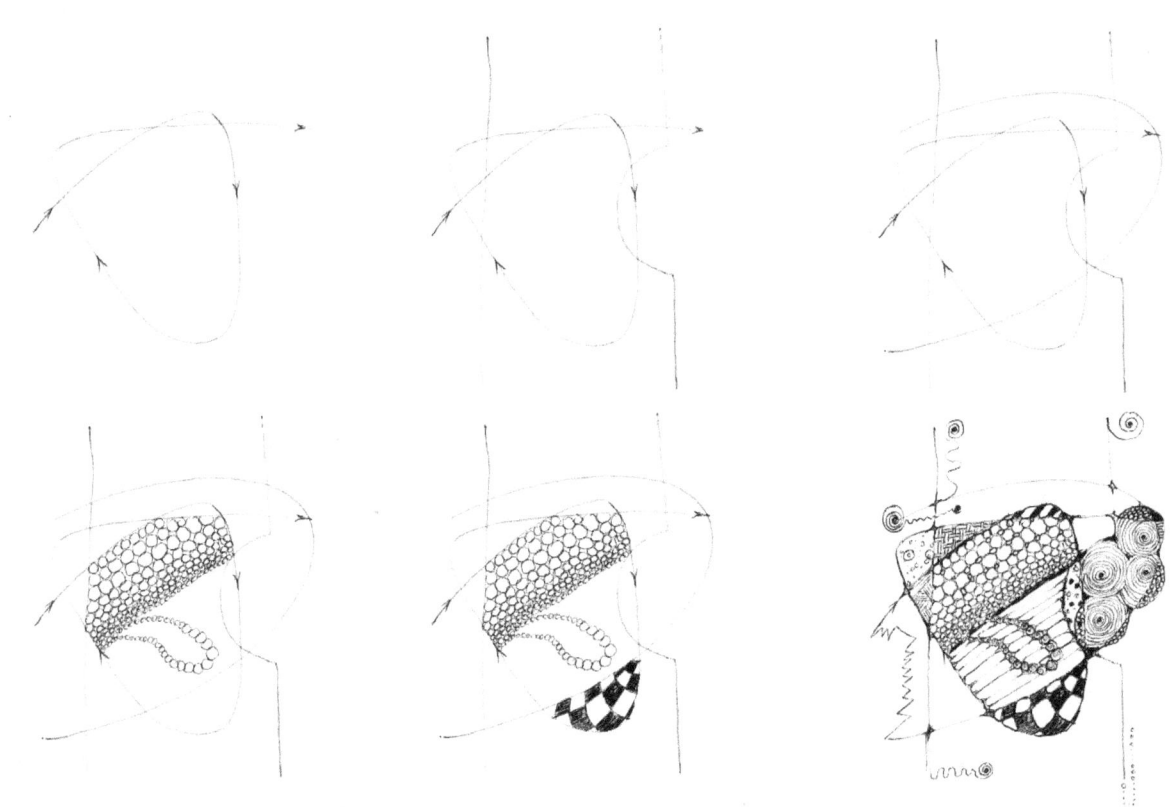

Imaginative NeoPopRealism Abstract ink pen/ pattern drawing. Visual step-by-step instruction

LESSON PLAN CONNECTION:

Once students are comfortable with the technique, it's time to discuss the fundamental question: "What are they attempting to accomplish?" What made these drawings art?

Many people argue this drawings express emotions more sincerely than traditional drawing styles. Art is an evocation of feelings. And in 21st century, many feel that the literal, representational artwork became marginalized and possibly even obsolete.

The next step in this lesson plan is to go back to the line and repetitive patterns, and draw NeoPopRealist abstract using the NeoPopRealism technique and imagination. Challenge students to reflect on music they listen, its rhythm, mood, and syncopation. Challenge them to use this drawing technique to communicate their feelings.

If students are having a hard time with this part of the lesson plan, make it specific. Ask them to write a feeling's name on the back of their paper: "Happy", "Angry", "Relaxed", "Frightened", "Sleepy", etc. How can they communicate that feeling? After they finished their drawings, have them look at each other's artwork and guess what feelings inspired their friends. Are they happy with their results? What could they improve?

RESOURCES:

-NeoPopRealism MOVIE #5 (2:00min) introduction to NeoPopRealism ink pen pattern drawing: http://goanimate.com/videos/0qwwEP0AaOew?utm_source=linkshare/

-Wall decals with NeoPopRealism ink pen drawings at 33% off for educators: www.neopoprealism.net

-Information on NeoPopRealism ink pen/ pattern drawing, its concept and Nadia Russ biography, who created this style in 1989: see page 101 and http://neopoprealismblackwhiteink.blogspot.com/

-A book "*How to Draw NeoPopRealism Abstract Images: Ink Backgrounds*", ISBN: 9780615527437

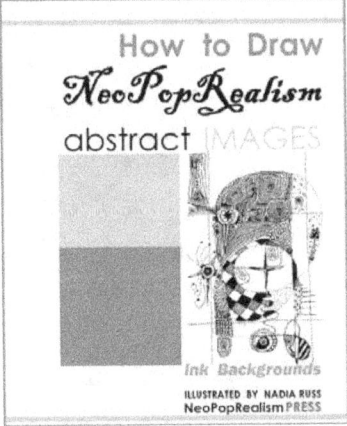

Art Lesson Plan 3

NeoPopRealism ink pen/ pattern drawing - Selfportrait

GRADES: 9-12, adapt. 3-5 and 6-8
TIME: Two 45-minute class periods
CONNECTIONS: Language Arts, Visual Arts, Technology

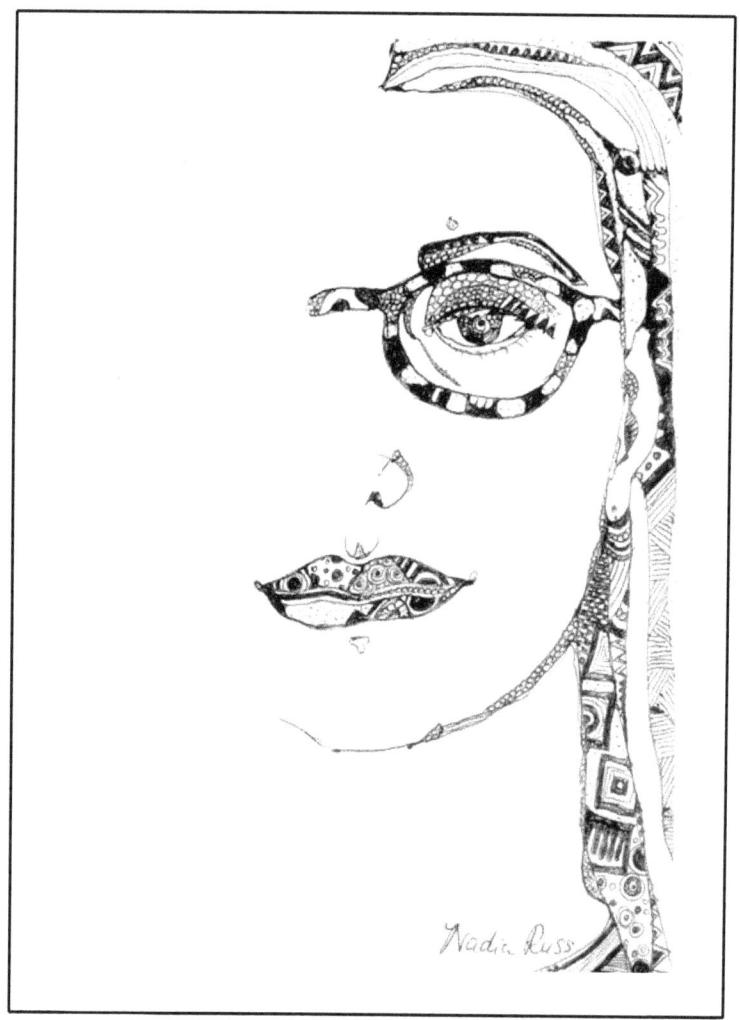

Nadia Russ, Selfportrait, ink pen/ paper, 2012

OBJECTIVES:
Students will:
- Examine Nadia Russ self-portraits and her biography to learn about the individual who created them. Consider how self-portraits aid the process of self-discovery.
- Explore NeoPopRealism ink pen pattern drawing style and concept that Nadia Russ created in 1989. If students are not familiar with this style yet, give the basics: A line creates shape, then this shape is divided into sections. Then, sections filled with different imaginative repetitive patterns, some sections should be left blank. Eraser never used because if a 'mistake' made it visually disappears after the new patterns balance the whole composition.
- Look attentively at drawings by Nadia Russ and old masters to respond to the questions and make comparisons about art styles NeoPopRealism and realism.
- Create selfportrait in NeoPopRealism ink pen pattern drawing manner.

MATERIALS:
- Computer to watch a fun Movie NeoPopRealism Introduction [1:32min]:
http://goanimate.com/videos/0K9HRf1_OMuY?utm_source=linkshare/
- A small mirrors that could be easily installed at a student's table at different angles (mirror preferable)
- Two sheets of white paper 8.5"x11"
- Ink pen black thin 0.7mm

LESSON IMPLEMENTATION:
Several days before the lesson begins tell students that they will need to bring in a mall mirror that could be easily installed at a student's table at different angles.

LESSON PLAN - ACTIVITY:
Day 1.
Class Period One.
Let students watch a fun Movie-NeoPopRealism Introduction [1:32min]:
http://goanimate.com/videos/0K9HRf1_OMuY?utm_source=linkshare/ .
Instruct students to read the biography of Nadia Russ in a book "*How to Draw Advanced NeoPopRealism Ink Images*", ISBN: 978-0615569758 , in page 101 of this book or at
http://neopoprealismblackwhiteink.blogspot.com/. Have students read and respond to questions and comparisons in the Nadia Russ Student Activities: A closer look and anatomy of Nadia Russ.
Introduce students NeoPopRealism ink pen pattern drawing style/concept. Discuss the Nadia Russ' self-portraits, emphasizing her use of ink pen - lines and patterns - to convey emotion.
Focus at repetitive patterns used in Nadia Russ' selfportraits, ask students to reproduce some of these patterns on white sheet of paper: zigzags, squares with circles inside, paralleled lines and strips, whirles, dots, more.
Remind students to bring a small mirror to the next class.

  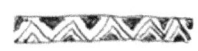  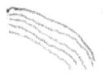

Some of repetitive patterns used in Nadia Russ' *Selfportrait*

Day 2.

Class Period Two

Remind students NeoPopRealism ink pen pattern drawing concept (see page 101). Have students make a Nadia Russ/ NeoPopRealism-style self-portrait using ink pen 0.7mm. Have them discuss their self-portraits and why they included each element-pattern, and what was difficult and easy. Have them describe their selfportraits in three words, and write these words on the back of a paper.

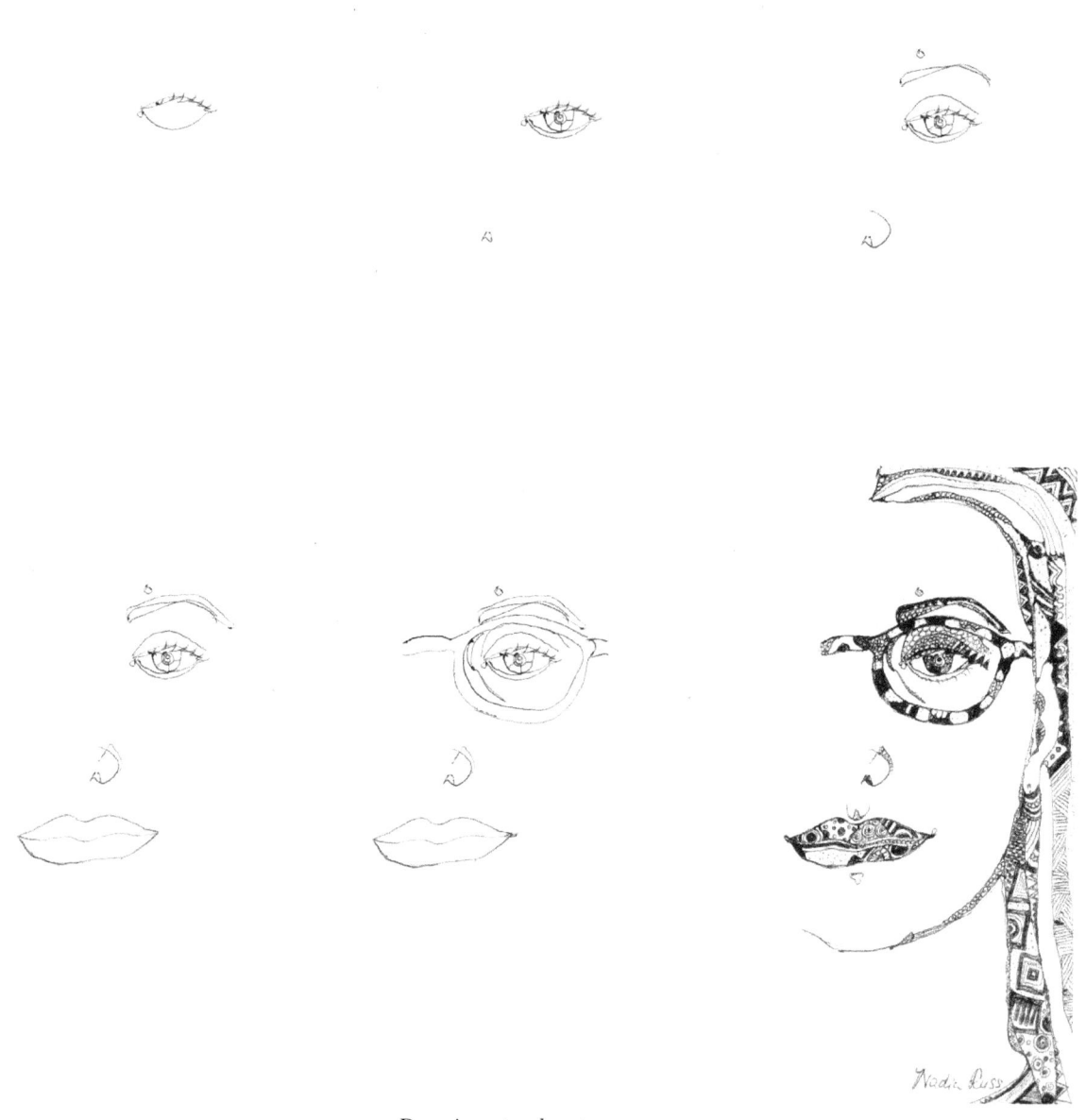

Drawing step-by-step

ASSESSMENT:
To evaluate students' Nadia Russ/ NeoPopRealism-style self-portraits, ask:

- Did the student use the line and repetitive patterns?
- Did the student use several repetitive patterns in the portrait? What kind?
- Does the self-portrait answer the question, Who am I?
- If the student made different-sided face self-portrait, do the two different sides of one face address the question, How am I changing from day to day?
- The three words on the back of each selfportrait should explain what the self-portrait communicates and should be supported by evidence in the work of art.

BACKGROUND INFORMATION:
Read Nadia Russ' brief biography: page 101 and http://neopoprealismblackwhiteink.blogspot.com.

RESOURCES:
1. A Movie NeoPopRealism Introduction [1:32min]:
http://goanimate.com/videos/0K9HRf1_OMuY?utm_source=linkshare/

2. Information on NeoPopRealism ink pen/ pattern drawing, its concept and Nadia Russ biography, who created this style in 1989: http://neopoprealismblackwhiteink.blogspot.com/

3. Nadia Russ' Selfportrait and other wall decals at 33% off to educators www.noprealism.net

4. A book "*How to Draw Advanced NeoPopRealism Ink Images*", ISBN: 978-0615569758 that contains a few teaching projects with step-by-step images and patterns drawing instructions, and everything you and students need to know to learn how to draw NeoPopRealism ink pen portrait.

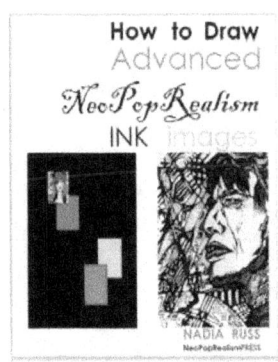

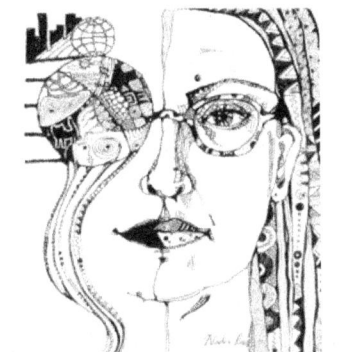

Nadia Russ, Selfportrait 2, ink/ paper

Art Lesson Plan 4

NeoPopRealism ink pen/ pattern drawing: A Cock

GRADES: 6-8. Adaptable for 9-12 and kindergarten, 3-5.
Visual Arts

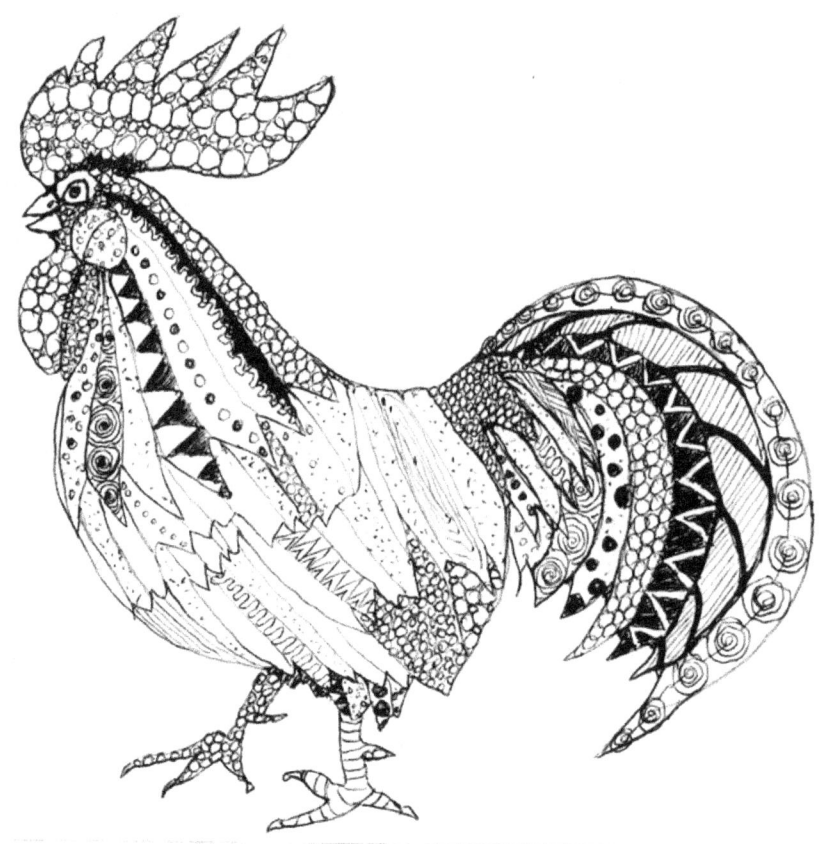

A Cock, NeoPopRealism ink pen / pattern drawing

OBJECTIVE
Students will:

1. Explore the NeoPopRealism art style concept and artist Nadia Russ biography who created it in 1989.

2. Compare and contrast realistic art and NeoPopRealism ink pen / pattern drawing..

3. Learn about NeoPopRealism ink pen/ pattern drawing (If student already know it, then, learn to draw the more imaginative and more complicated-exotic repetitive patterns).

4. Create a drawing "*A Cock*", combining realistic drawing (contour of a cock) and imaginative drawing (repetitive patterns).

MATERIALS:
- 8.5"x11" white drawing paper
- Ink pen black 0.7mm

PREPARATION:
Display some of Nadia RUSS' art posters in the classroom (purchase them from online store, see Resources below). Have a presentation ready to show students Nadia Russ' NeoPopRealism art.

LESSON PROCEDURE:
Day 1:
1. Introduce (or remind) Nadia RUSS' biography and concept of NeoPopRealism style of visual arts and ink pen/ pattern drawing to students. Compare Nadia Russ' ink pen /pattern artworks and pencil drawings by Leonardo Da Vinci. Discuss how they are similar and different.

2. Show photographs of 3-4 different cocks, discuss the structure of the cock's body and his characteristics.

3. Have students write their names on the back of 8.5"x11" paper. Demonstrate how to draw step-by-step an image of a cock using NeoPopRealism ink pen / pattern drawing concept: a line creates a contour of an image and sections. Then, these sections filled with different repetitive patterns, some leave blank. Eraser is never used.

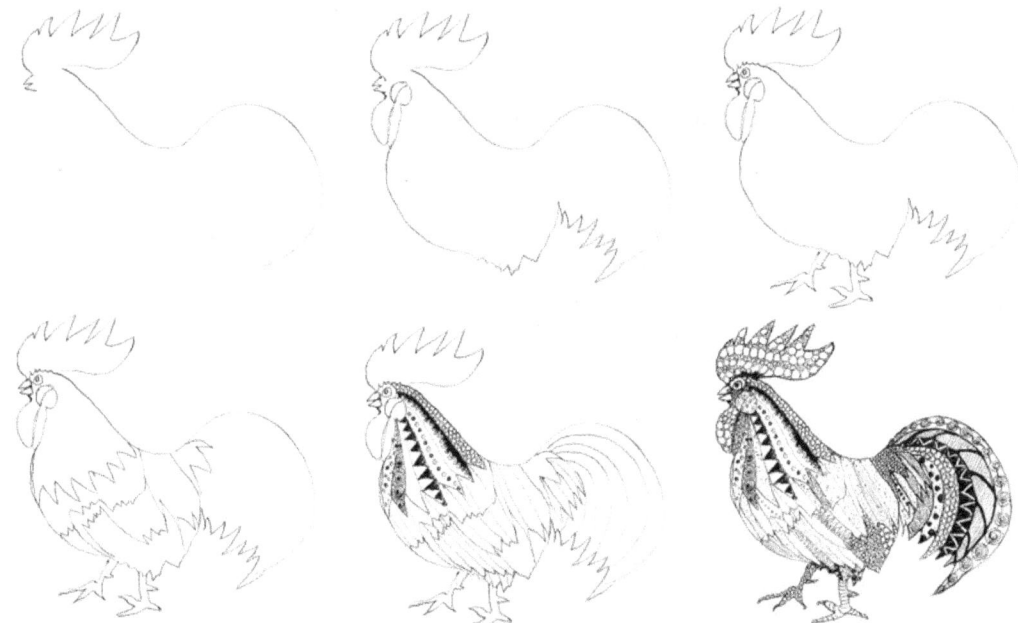

NeoPopRealism ink pen/ pattern drawing step-by-step: A Cock

Day 2:

4. Continue teaching how to draw simple or more complicated imaginative repetitive patterns: zigzags, strips, lines, waves, triangles (black and blank), dots, whirles, circles (black and blank), etc., their combinations in different variations. Offer students two sheets of white paper divided into squares 1,5 inch each and ask to fill each square-section with different imaginative repetitive pattern.

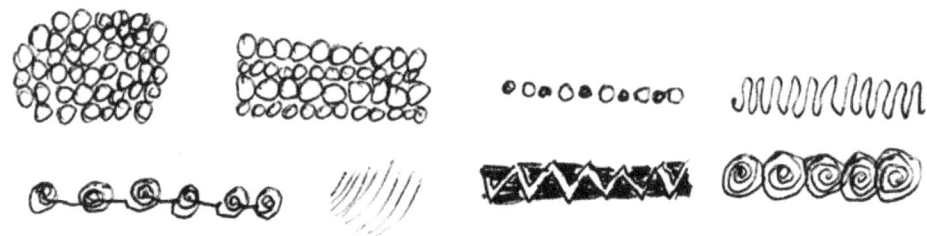

Repetitive patterns used in a drawing A Cock

Day 3:

5. Offer students to create a Cock from the beginning to end using more imaginative repetitive patterns. Present students 10 NeoPopRealism canons for happier life (see page 101 and at www.nadiaruss.com) and let they explain each canon how they understand them.

Repeat with students the NeoPopRealism ink pen pattern drawing concept: a line creates shapes and sections; then, these sections filled with different repetitive patterns, some left blank. Eraser never used. Compare students' work, discuss differences.

RESOURCES (links):

1.Wall decals with NeoPopRealism ink pen drawings at 33% off for educators: www.neopoprealism.net

2. Information on NeoPopRealism ink pen/ pattern drawing, its concept and Nadia Russ biography, who created this drawing style in 1989 see in page 101 and in http://neopoprealismblackwhiteink.blogspot.com/

Art Lesson Plan 5

NeoPopRealism Ink Pen/ Pattern Drawing - Exotic Flower & Butterfly

GRADES: 9-12, adaptable 3-5, 6-8
Visual art and technology

This lesson plan takes inspiration from Nadia RUSS' art. Notice the strong contour and patterns' lines in these composition. This would be a wonderful unit to try integrating "man and his environment".

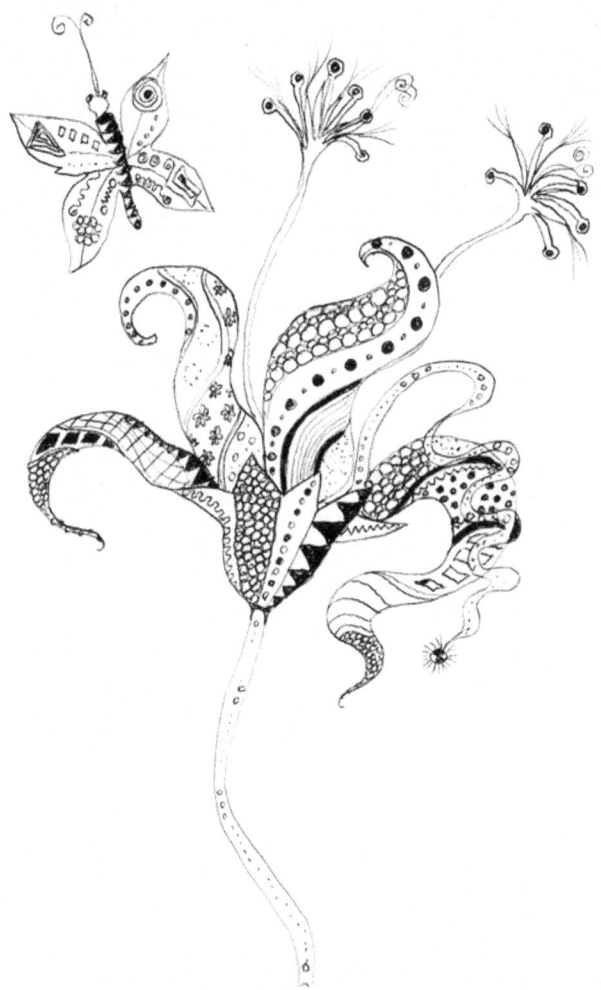

Exotic Flower and Butterfly

OBJECTIVES:
Students will
-learn about NeoPopRealism ink pen / pattern drawing style and its creator Nadia Russ
-develop skills in imaginative drawing - draw from their mind
-develop skills in drawing the flowing whimsical lines and a variety of patterns
-learn a full values of contrast of black and white
-meditate.

MATERIALS:
-Computer to watch a short film-dialog [2:00min] introduction to NeoPopRealism:
http://goanimate.com/videos/0sCUFTuM0Yyw/1/
-Ink pen thin black 0.7mm
-Drawing paper white

INSTRUCTION/MOTIVATION:
Review principles/concept of NeoPopRealism ink pen/ pattern drawing: a line creates sections. Then, these sections filled with different repetitive patterns, some section(s) left blank. Eraser never used. Demonstrate step-by-step technique of drawing line, creating sections, and filling sections with different patterns.

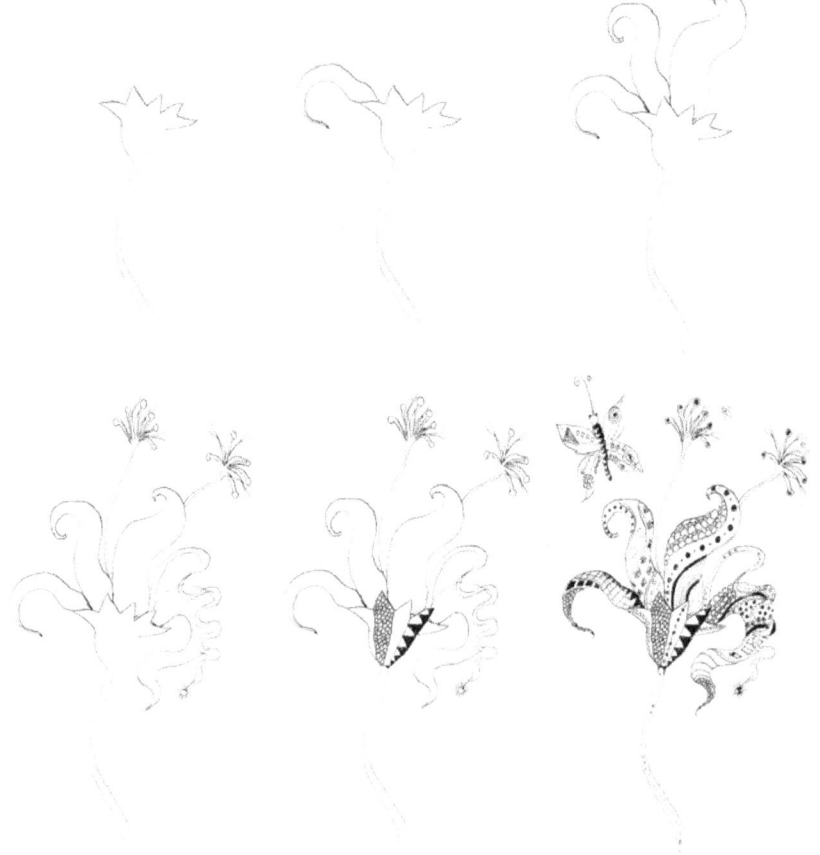

Exotic Flower drawing step-by-step

In this lesson, you teach a fun way to make an original NeoPopRealism ink pen / pattern drawings on a small scale.

Display some of Nadia RUSS' art posters in the classroom and show her work online. Have a presentation ready to students. When drawing process begins, you can turn on music (not loud), preferably jazz. NeoPopRealism ink pen/ pattern drawing is meditative, it is drawing from within, when artist expresses his moods, feelings, his inner world. If a 'mistake' made it will disappear with the following repetitive patterns that will balance the whole composition and would make a 'mistake' invisible.

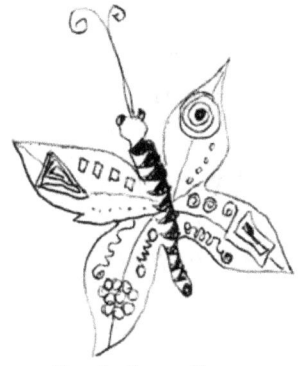

Exotic Butterfly

LESSON PLAN - BACKGROUND and HISTORICAL INFORMATION:

Nadia RUSS is a Ukrainian-born Russian painter/graphic artist living in the USA, who created in 1989 a style of visual arts NeoPopRealism, she is famous for creating in 1989 this innovative meditative ink pen / pattern drawing style. Instead of careful copying reality, the wild life or human figure she creates her artwork using her imagination.

PROCEDURE:

1. Select subject matter for the drawing: exotic flower and butterfly, the objects that will have beautiful form and interesting texture. Discuss the characteristics of exotic butterfly, its shape, structure, parts of the body, texture.
2. With whimsical lines draw contour of an exotic flower.
3. Divide petals of a flower into sections.
4. Fill sections with different repetitive patterns: circles, dots, zigzags, squares, waves, more.
5. Draw contour of a butterfly above the flower; divide its wings into sections.
6. Fill wings' sections with different patterns: circles, squares, triangle, waves, more.
7. Explain students NeoPopRealism ink pen pattern drawing concept, have them practice.
8. Critique the work at the end.

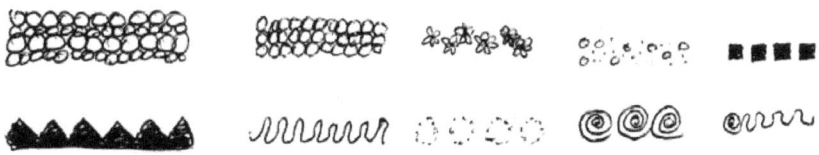

Repetitive patterns used in a drawing Exotic Flower

EVALUATION:

Did students create an interesting composition using their imagination - show skills in whimsical line and repetitive patterns drawing?

RESOURCES:

1. Wall decals with NeoPopRealism ink pen drawings at 33% off for educators: www.neopoprealism.net

2. NeoPopRealism short online Jr.Movie-introduction: http://goanimate.com/videos/0sCUFTuM0Yyw/1/

3. The procedures of drawing butterflies, flowers and repetitive patterns can be found in a book "*NeoWhimsies: NeoPopRealism Ink Drawing Basics for Mannequins*", ISBN: 978-0615651859

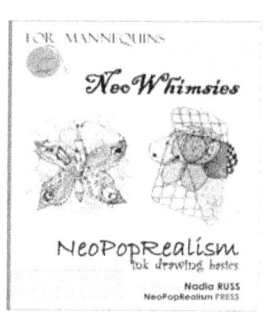

Art Lesson Plan 6

NeoPopRealism Ink Pen / Pattern Drawing "Faces" Inspired by Nadia Russ

GRADES: 6-8, 9-12
SUBJECT: Visual Arts and Music, Arts and Technology

Includes NeoPopRealism Jr. Movie-Introduction [2:00min]. See Resources below.

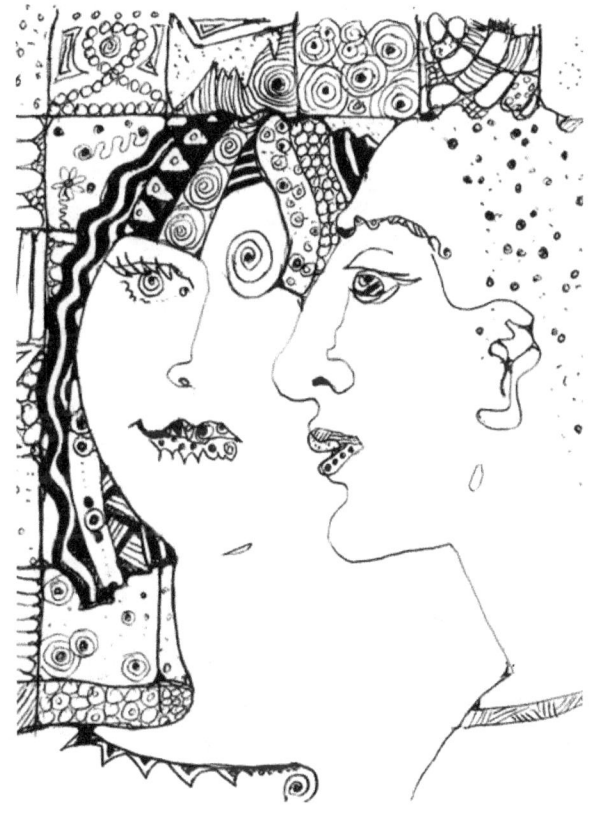

OBJECTIVE
Students will:
1. Explore NeoPopRealism art style, ink pen pattern drawing concept and artist Nadia Russ, NeoPopRealism art style creator biography.
2. Compare and contrast realistic art and NeoPopRealism.
3. Create NeoPopRealism ink pen/ pattern drawing "Faces" inspired by Nadia Russ.

MATERIALS:
- Computer with internet access to watch a short fun movie NeoPopRealism intro
-A book "*How to Draw NeoPopRealism Ink Images: Basics*", ISBN: 978-0615515755
- 8.5"x11" white drawing paper
- black ink pen thin 0.77mm

PREPARATION:
Display some of Nadia RUSS' art posters in the classroom. Have a presentation ready to show students Nadia Russ' NeoPopRealism art. See RESOURCES.

LESSON PROCEDURE:
1. Day 1: Explore NeoPopRealism style of visual arts and Nadia RUSS' life with students. See page 101, use a book ISBN: 978-0615515755 that contains the introduction and other important

27

information, and website http://neopoprealismblackwhiteink.blogspot.com/. Compare Nadia Russ' ink pen / pattern drawing portraits and pencil drawings by Rembrandt. Discuss how they are similar and different.

2. Hand out 8.5"x11" papers and have students write their names on the back.

Turn on music (not loud), preferably jazz. Demonstrate how to draw step-by-step NeoPopRealism ink pen / pattern drawing "Faces". Draw the contour of a man's profile, eye, nose. Then, draw face of a woman.- eye, hair, nose, lips. Then, divide woman's hair into sections and the background into squares. Fill appeared sections with different repetitive patterns.

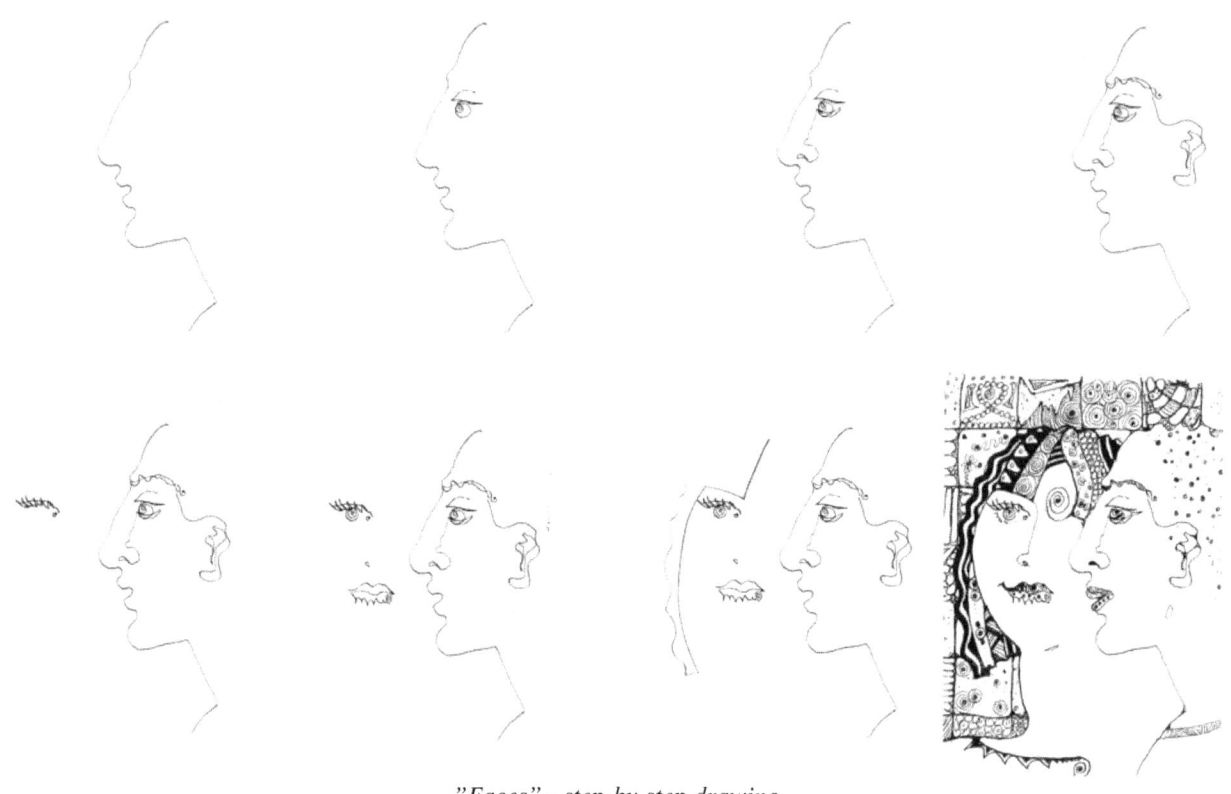

"Faces" - step-by step drawing

3. Day 2: Continue teaching drawing different repetitive patterns. A book "How to Draw NeoPopRealism Ink Images: Basics", ISBN: 978-0615515755 contains special chapter that offer student pages-Gallery with sections to fill them with different imaginative patterns. As an option student can draw patterns on a spare sheet of paper, divided into 1,5 inch squares. Drawing patterns is meditative process, students achieve purity of heir mind, this drawing stimulates creativity.

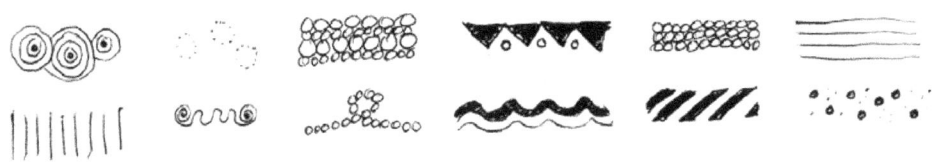

Repetitive patterns used in a drawing "Faces"

4. Day 3: Demonstrate how drawing the different repetitive patterns can change the whole meaning of artwork and its character. Offer students to complete artworks - the images-templates of faces in a book "*How to Draw NeoPopRealism Ink Images: Basics*", ISBN: 978-0615515755, filling sections with different imaginative patterns.

5. Day 4: Offer students to draw the NeoPopRealist images of faces from beginning to end on special pages of a book "*How to Draw NeoPopRealism Ink Images: Basics*", ISBN: 978-0615515755. As an option they can draw on white paper 8.5"x11". Explore with students 10 NeoPopRealism canons for happier life. (Canons can be found in this book on page 101 and in www.NadiaRuss.com).

6. Day 5. Discuss with students the NeoPopRealism ink pen pattern drawing concept that Nadia Russ created in 1989: a line creates sections; then, these sections filled with different repetitive patterns seemed unpredictable and asymmetrically. Eraser never used; this drawing is meditative.

RESOURCES:

1. Information on NeoPopRealism ink pen/ pattern drawing, its concept and Nadia Russ biography, who created this style in 1989 in this book see page 101 and in http://neopoprealismblackwhiteink.blogspot.com/

2. Wall decals with NeoPopRealism ink pen drawings at 33% off for educators: www.neopoprealism.net

3. NeoPopRealism' short (fun) online Jr.Movie-introduction [2:00min]: http://goanimate.com/videos/0qwwEP0AaOew?utm_source=linkshare

4. Nadia Russ' official website: www.nadiaaruss.com

5. A book "*How to Draw NeoPopRealism Ink Images: Basics*", ISBN: 978-0615515755 that contains the teaching projects with step-by-step images and patterns drawing instructions, templates, the patterns' gallery to fill out, special pages for drawing, NeoPopRealism background and history, Nadia Russ biography, 10 NeoPopRealism canons for happier life, more.

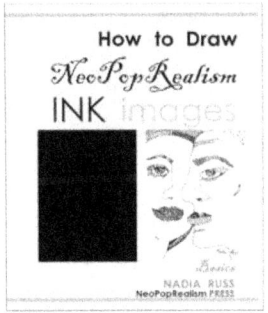

Art Lesson Plan 7

The (Fallen) Leaves, NeoPopRealism Ink Pen/ Pattern Drawing Inspired by Nadia Russ

GRADES: 3-5, 6-8, and high school
SUBJECT: Art: NeoPopRealism ink pen/ pattern drawing and music

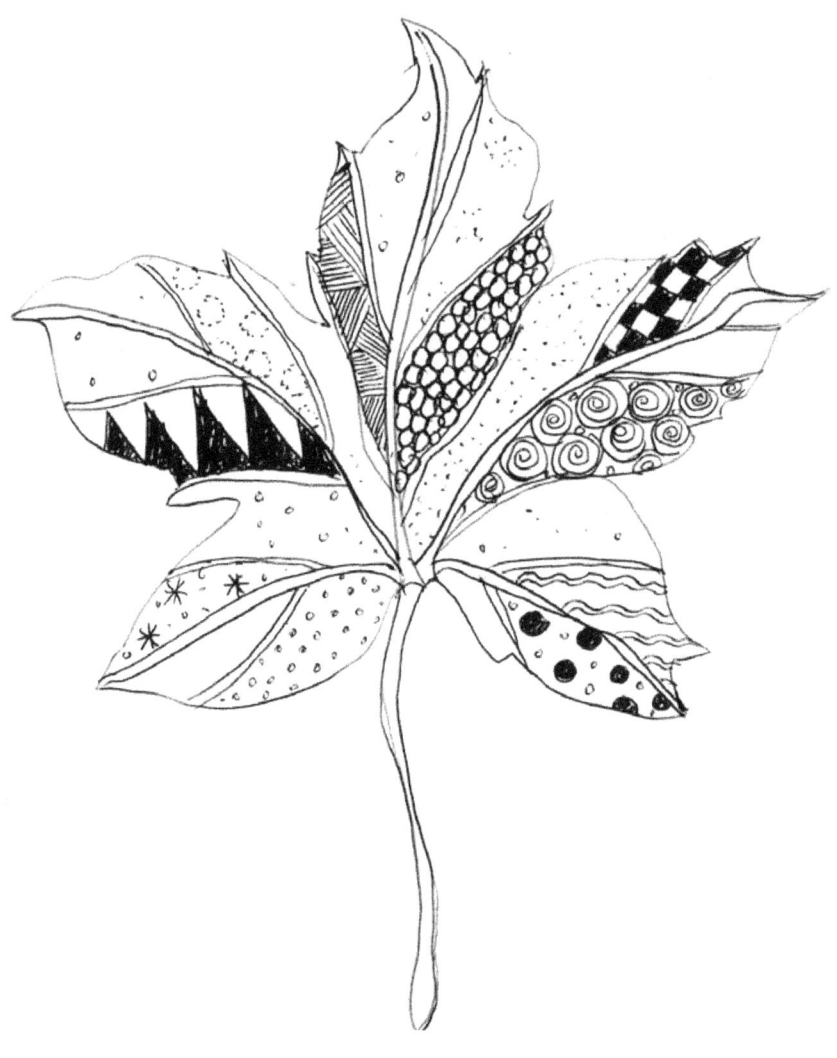

A (Fallen) Leaf

DESCRIPTION:

In this lesson, students will draw over leaves to create images of falling leaves using line and different imaginative repetitive patterns. This lesson plan takes inspiration from Nadia RUSS' art and NeoPopRealism art style that she created in 1989. Students will be able to define the terms "NeoPopRealism" and "meditative ink pattern drawing" and differentiate these from Realism and other styles approaches.

GOALS:

Students will learn
- about NeoPopRealism and this style creator Nadia Russ
- make a picture of falling leaves; draw over leaves, adding to realistic drawing the imaginative elements, such as repetitive patterns.

MATERIALS:

Different types of leaves.
Cardstock white paper 8.5"x11".
Ink pen thin black 0.7mm

LESSON PLAN - MOTIVATION:

In this lesson, you teach a fun and easy way to make realistic and imaginative at the same time images of leaves - original NeoPopRealism ink pattern drawings on a small scale. The technique is appropriate for students of kindergarten and up. It is also fun for adults to make these kind NeoPopRealism ink pen / pattern drawings. Display some of Nadia RUSS' art posters in the classroom or show her work online. Have a presentation ready to students. When drawing process begins, you can turn on music (not loud), preferably jazz.

NeoPopRealism ink pen/ pattern drawing is meditative. The meditative state of mind is the highest state in which our mind can exists. When students draw NeoPopRealism ink patterns their mind is open for renewal. This art style's creator Nadia Russ explains NeoPopRealism pattern drawling as the work from within, when artist expresses his/her inner world. You need no eraser, because if a 'mistake' made it would disappear with the following repetitive patterns that would balance the whole composition and would make a 'mistake' invisible.

LESSON PLAN - BACKGROUND and HISTORICAL INFORMATION:

Nadia RUSS is a Ukrainian-born Russian painter/ graphic artist living in the USA. She is famous for innovative NeoPopRealism and meditative ink pattern drawing style. Instead of careful copying reality - wild life or human figure, Nadia RUSS creates her artwork using imagination. As Nadia RUSS experimented and developed her distinctive techniques, her art became more symbolic. For her NeoPopRealism ink pen / pattern drawings she uses mostly white paper and black ink pen.

How did Nadia RUSS develop her unique and original style NeoPopRealism? RUSS had studied classical drawing and composition since she was a child, but later she found herself drawn to produce more imaginative artwork. In 1989, she created NeoPopRealism art style and ink pattern drawing concept: line creates sections; then, these section filled with different repetitive patterns, some section should be left blank. If artwork made on canvas using color paints and brushes, then, it will be a combination of sections filled with hot and cold color paint, partly with patterns. In 1990, Nadia RUSS exhibited her first ink/ pattern drawings in a group exhibition in Moscow's famous Manege. Later, she exhibited her artwork in art galleries. In 1996, she moved to the Bahamas, where her artwork gained special brightness. In 2000, she came to the USA, where she lives till present. Nadia Russ created a term "NeoPopRealism" January 4, 2003. Same year, she manifested her new style of visual arts NeoPopRealism internationally. In 2004, RUSS created NeoPopRealism 10 canons for happier life. In 2006-2007, several US and European museums collected Nadia Russ' paintings and drawings and now, these artworks are in their permanent collections.

Ask students to bring leaves that they find on their way to school.

PROCEDURE:
Day 1:
1. Introduce Nadia RUSS' life and NeoPopRealism style of visual arts to students, see in this book page 101 and http://neopoprealismblackwhiteink.blogspot.com/. Compare Nadia Russ' ink/pattern drawing and pencil drawings by Leonardo DaVinci. Discuss how they are similar and different.

2. Turn on music. Demonstrate how to draw step-by-step a leaf - NeoPopRealism ink pen/ pattern image - starting with the contour and ending with the drawing repetitive patterns. Demonstrate how different repetitive patterns can change the image's character.
Ask students to draw the realistic part of a leaf on a piece of paper.

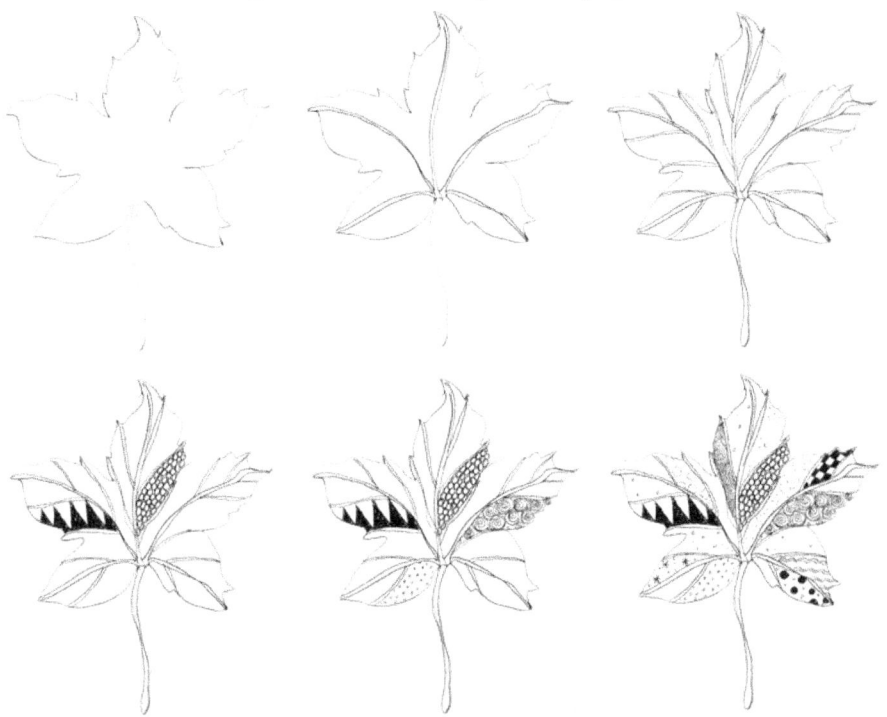

Step-by-step drawing the leaf

3. Day
2: Continue teaching the drawing of a leaf. Students focus on creating the repetitive patterns, filling with them the sections of a leaf (see illustration).

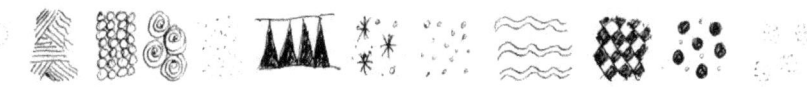

The repetitive patterns used in a drawing

Drawing patterns is meditative process. When you draw patterns, imagination is used, it is unconscious process. When finished, offer student discuss NeoPopRealism art style drawing concept and compare their work.

RESOURCES:

-Wall decals with NeoPopRealism ink pen drawings at 33% off for educators: www.neopoprealism.net

-Information on NeoPopRealism, the ink pen/ pattern drawing concept, Nadia Russ biography, who created this style in 1989, and NeoPopRealism 10 canons for happier life see in this book's page 101 and in http://neopoprealismblackwhiteink.blogspot.com/

-Nadia Russ Official website: www.nadiaruss.com

Art Lesson Plan 8

NeoWhimsies Letters - NeoPopRealist Ink Pen / Pattern Drawing Inspired by Nadia Russ: First Initial Letters

Adaptable ALL GRADES
Art & Music

OBJECTIVES:
Students will
- explore NeoPopRealism ink pen pattern drawing concept and work of artist Nadia Russ who created this style in 1989 (see page 101 and Resources).
- define the terms "NeoPopRealism" and "NeoWhimsies"; differentiate NeoPopRealism/ NeoWhimsies drawing with its contrasting and flatness from realism approach.
- learn that NeoWhimsies are the simplified NeoPopRealism ink pen pattern drawings.
- experiment with the drawing the repetitive patterns
- create a letter inspired by the drawings by Nadia Russ, using ink pen and white paper.

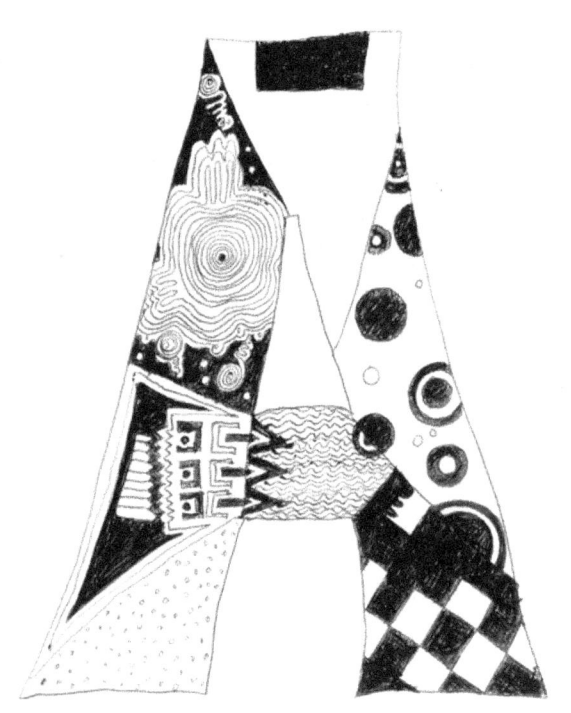

MATERIALS:
-ink pen black 0.7mm
-8.5"x11" white paper (2)

LESSON ACTIVITIES:

Day 1:
Display in classroom posters with Nadia Russ' NeoPopRealism ink pen pattern drawings (see Resources below). Introduce (or remind) the NeoPopRealism ink pen pattern drawing concept and

artist Nadia Russ' biography, who created this style in 1989; see page 101 and http://neopoprealismblackwhiteink.blogspot.com/.

Ask students to compare drawings by Nadia Russ and drawings by old master Leonardo da Vinci.

Discuss with students the Alphabet and languages and why people need alphabet - every language has its alphabet: English, French, Russian, German, other.

Prepare ink pen and paper for all students.

Each student will create one letter, an initial of his/her first name.

Demonstrate the drawing of a letter *A*. Using line creates its shape. Then, divide it asymmetrically into sections. Then, fill appeared sections with different repetitive patterns: circles, dots, whirles, lines, zigzags, waves, some leave blank. Explain why drawing NeoPopRealism/ NeoWhimsies needs no eraser: if a 'mistake' made, it visually disappears because the following patterns make this 'mistake' invisible and the whole composition balanced. Discuss contrast and flatness.

Offer students sheets of 8.5"x11" paper, divided into squares/section and turn on music (not loud, preferable jazz). Offer students create in each square/ section different repetitive pattern. Drawing patterns is meditative process.

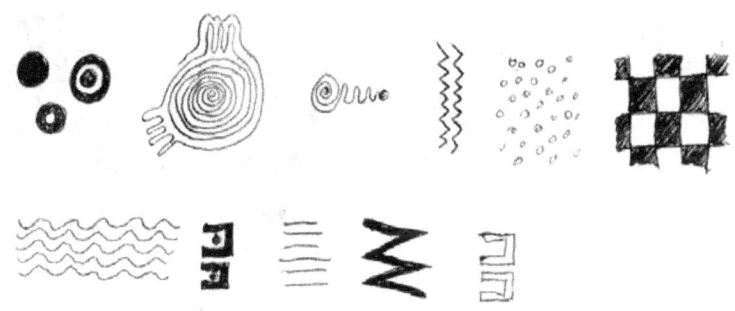

Repetitive patterns used in letter 'A'

Day 2:

Remind students the NeoPopRealism/ NeoWhimsies ink pen/ pattern drawing concept: A line creates sections, then these sections filled with different repetitive patterns, some sections left blank. Eraser never used. NeoWhimsies are the simplified NeoPopRealism ink pen/ pattern drawings. Turn on music (not loud). Students draw the shapes of the letters. Suggest to draw the big letter. Then, they divide the shape of a letter into sections and fill each section with different pattern, some section(s) should be left blank.

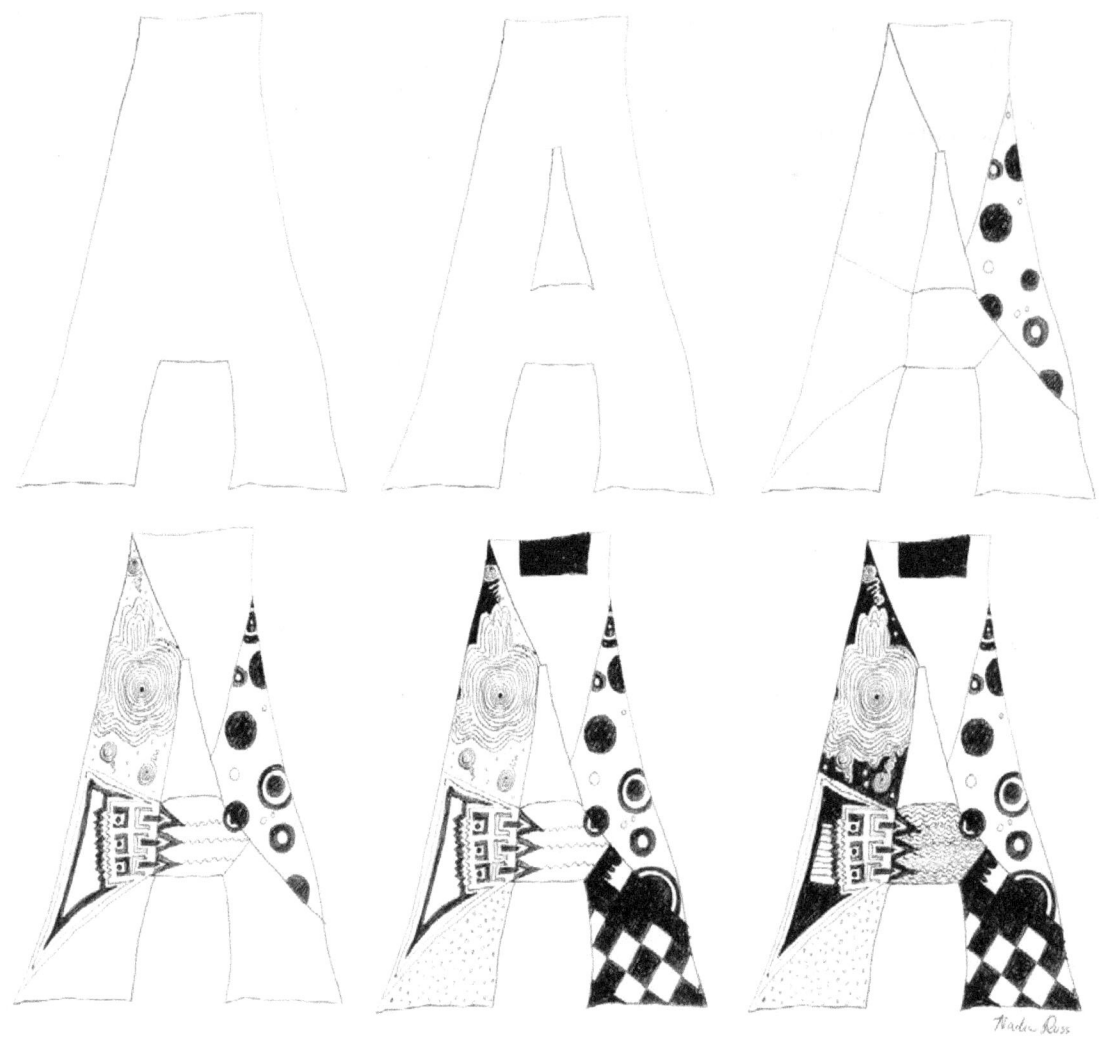

Drawing step-by-step

When work is finished, the students compare and discuss their letters, they discuss NeoPopRealism/ NeoWhimsies ink pen pattern drawing concept and patterns they used in drawings. Students define the terms "NeoPopRealism" and "NeoWhimsy".

RESOURCES:

Information on NeoPopRealism ink pen/ pattern drawing, its concept and artist Nadia Russ biography, who created this style in 1989, see in page 101 and in http://neopoprealismblackwhiteink.blogspot.com/

Wall decals with NeoPopRealism ink pen drawings at 33% off for educators: www.neopoprealism.net

Art Lesson Plan 9

NeoPopRealism Ink Pen/ Pattern Drawing: A Halloween Mask for a Short Video
"The Dancing Monsters and Ghosts"

GRAGES: 6-8, adapt. 3-5, 9-12
SUBJECT: Visual Arts, Crafts, Language Arts, Music
TIME: Three 45-minute class periods

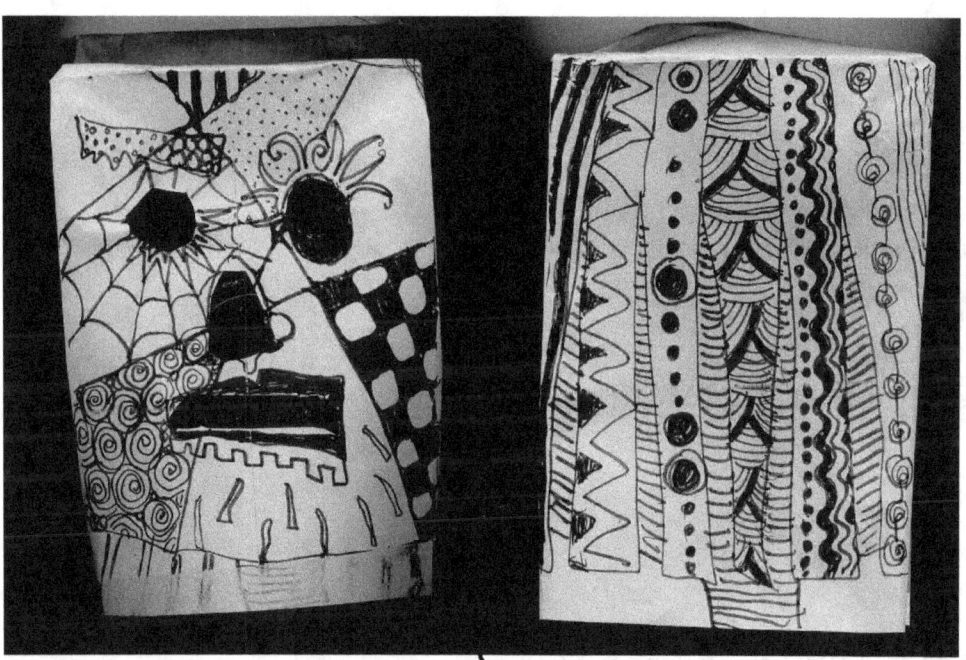

HALLOWEEN MASK-FRONT\HALLOWEEN MASK-BACK

OBJECTIVES:
Students will
- learn a brief history of Halloween.
- examine NeoPopRealist Halloween Mask.
- learn (or be reminded) about NeoPopRealism ink pen pattern drawing style and concept that Nadia Russ created in 1989: A line creates shape, then this shape is divided into sections. Then, sections filled with different imaginative repetitive patterns, some sections should be left blank. Eraser never used because if a 'mistake' made it visually disappears after new patterns balance the

whole composition (see page 101 and http://neopoprealismblackwhiteink.blogspot.com/).

- compare the traditional Halloween Masks and NeoPopRealism Halloween ink pen/ pattern Mask to respond to questions and make comparisons about art styles NeoPopRealism and Realism.

- create a new monster Mask in the NeoPopRealism ink pen/ pattern drawing manner for a scary movie "*NeoPopRealist Halloween: The Dancing Monsters and Ghosts*".

- create and write a name of the monster and a story about how this monster scary people, about favorite things it eats, what it likes to do.

- brainstorm to think of and list the supernatural creatures, classify them by size and habits.

- students dance with the NeoPopRealism Halloween Masks they created on their heads, expressing the Monsters' characters. Music can be found online. Teacher tapes a short movie (10 min. or less) "*NeoPopRealist Halloween: The Dancing Monsters and Ghosts*" of this collective dance and posts this film on Youtube.com.

MATERIALS:
- Middle size brown paper bag (regularly it can be found in supermarkets and other stores)
- Two sheets of white paper 8.5"x11"
- Black ink pen 0.7 mm.
- Black thick marker
- Scissors
- Small digital camera to tape 7-10 min movie
- Computer or player to play Halloween dance music

LESSON IMPLEMENTATION:
Several days before the lesson begins tell students that they will need to bring in a middle size brown paper bag that will be used for creating the Halloween Mask.

LESSON ACTIVITIES:

Day 1.
Class Period One:
Tell students a brief history of Halloween (see page 41).
Examine the NeoPopRealism Halloween Mask:
Instruct students about NeoPopRealism ink pen pattern drawing style and its concept, about Nadia Russ (brief biography), who created this style in 1989 (see pages 40, 101, and http://neopoprealismblackwhiteink.blogspot.com/).
Examine the traditional drawings of the Halloween Masks (find them online).
Have students respond to questions and make comparisons how traditional masks are different from the NeoPopRealist Halloween Mask, emphasizing use of ink pen - lines and patterns - to convey the character and emotion.
Focus on the repetitive patterns used in NeoPopRealist Halloween Mask, ask students to create patterns using ink pen 0.7 mm on separate white sheet of paper: the paralleled lines and strips, zigzags, squares, circles, whirles, dots, their combinations and variations.

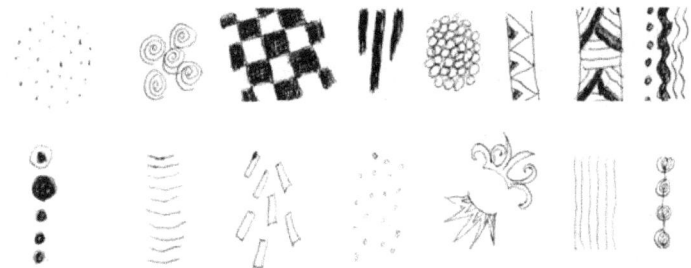

Repetitive patterns used in the NeoPopRealist Halloween Mask

Remind students to bring a middle size brown paper bag to the next class.

Day 2.
Class Period Two:
Explore with students the NeoPopRealism ink pen/ pattern drawing concept (see Lesson Plan - Background and Historical Information and page 101): a line creates sections, then these sections filled with different repetitive patterns.

Have students create a monster's Mask in the NeoPopRealism ink pen/ pattern drawing manner for a scary movie "*NeoPopRealist's Halloween: The Dancing Monsters and Ghosts*". Have students cut two holes in areas of eyes, one hole for nose to breathe, and one - in area of mouth. Then, have students divide the brown bag into sections and fill these sections with different repetitive patterns using black marker. Some section should be left blank. Students will create the NeoPopRealist Halloween masks using their imagination and different kinds of repetitive patterns.

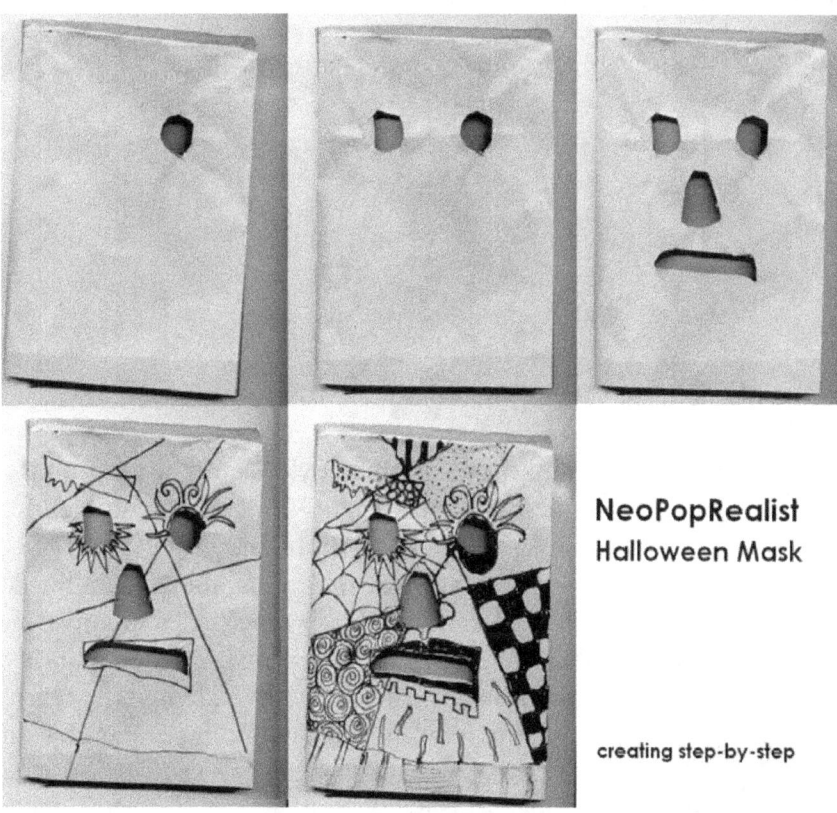

NeoPopRealist
Halloween Mask

creating step-by-step

39

Have them discuss why they included each element-pattern, and what was difficult and easy while creating a NeoPopRealism Halloween Mask. Have them describe their Masks in three words.

Day 3.
Class Period Three:
Have students create and write on white paper a name of the monster they created, a brief story about the experience a monster has in scarring people, favorite thing it eats, what it likes to do. List and classify the supernatural creatures in different ways.

Have students wear their recently created NeoPopRealist Halloween Masks. Turn on the music. Ask students to dance, expressing characters of the monsters' Masks they are wearing.

Teacher tapes a short (maximum 10 min) movie called "*NeoPopRealist's Halloween: The Dancing Monsters and Ghosts*". Teacher posts this film on Youtube.com.

LESSON PLAN - BACKGROUND and HISTORICAL INFORMATION:
Nadia Russ & NeoPopRealism:
Nadia RUSS is a Ukrainian-born Russian painter/ graphic artist living in the USA, who created a style of visual arts NeoPopRealism. She is famous for innovative NeoPopRealism art and ink pen pattern drawing, including abstract, the meditative style that she created in 1989. Instead of careful copying reality - wild life or human figure, Nadia RUSS creates her artwork using imagination. As Nadia RUSS experimented and developed her distinctive techniques, her drawings became more symbolic. For her drawings she uses white paper and black ink pen. However, sometimes, she uses blue ink on white paper and gold/silver ink on black paper - http://neopoprealismblackwhiteink.blogspot.com/.

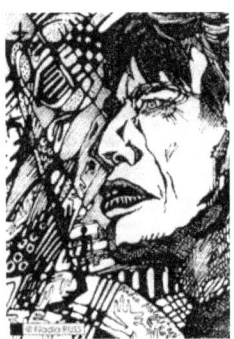

Nadia Russ, Mick Jagger, NeoPopRealism, ink & pen on paper, 1994

How did Nadia RUSS develop her unique and original style NeoPopRealism? RUSS had studied classical drawing and composition since she was a child, but as she studied she found herself drawn to produce less realistic, more imaginative artwork. In 1989, she created NeoPopRealism art style and ink pattern drawing concept: line creates sections; then, these section filled with different repetitive patterns, some section should be left blank. If artwork made on canvas using color paints and a brush, then, it would be a combination of sections filled with hot and cold color paint, partly with patterns. In 1990, RUSS exhibited her first ink/ pattern drawings in a group exhibition in Moscow's famous Manege. Later, she was exhibiting her artwork in art galleries. In 1996, she moved to the Freeport, Bahamas, where her artwork gained special brightness. In 2000, she came to the USA where she lives till present. Nadia Russ create a term "NeoPopRealism" January 4, 2003. Same year, she manifested her new style of visual arts NeoPopRealism internationally. In 2004, she created NeoPopRealism 10 canons for happier life. In 2006-2007, several US and European museums collected Nadia Russ' paintings and drawings and now, these artworks are in the permanent collections of these museums.

ABOUT HALLOWEEN

Halloween is a time of superstition and celebration. It is thought to have originated with the ancient Celtic festival of Samhain (pronounced sow-in). Then, people would wear costumes and light bonfires to ward off the ghosts. Pope Gregory III (8th century) designated 1st of November as a time to honor all saints and martyrs. The evening before was known as All Hallows' Eve and later Halloween. Halloween evolved into a community-based event with child-friendly activities, such as trick-or-treating. Around the world, people usher in the winter season with costumes and sweet treats.

The Celts, who lived 2,000 years ago in the area that is now Ireland, the UK and northern France, celebrated their new year on 1st of November. This is the end of summer and the beginning of a time of year that was often associated with human death. Celts celebrated Samhain on the night of October 31, when it was believed that the ghosts of the dead returned to earth. Celts thought that the presence of the otherworldly spirits made it easier for the Druids or Celtic priests, to make predictions about the future.

The American Halloween tradition of trick-or-treating dates back to the All Souls' Day parades in England. Then, poor people would beg for food and the rich would give them the "soul cakes" in return for their promise to pray for their dead relatives. It was encouraged by the church as a way to replace the ancient practice of leaving food and wine for roaming spirits.

The tradition of dressing in costumes for Halloween has Celtic and European roots. Hundreds of years ago, winter was the frightening time. On Halloween, to avoid being recognized by the ghosts, people would wear masks when they left their homes after dark so that the ghosts would mistake them for fellow spirits. To keep ghosts away from their houses on Halloween, people would place bowls of food outside their homes to prevent them from attempting to enter...

RESOURCES:

1. Information on NeoPopRealism ink pen/ pattern drawing, its concept and Nadia Russ biography, who created this style in 1989: http://neopoprealismblackwhiteink.blogspot.com/

2. Wall decals with NeoPopRealism ink pen drawings at 33% off for educators: www.neopoprealism.net

3. A book "*How to Draw NeoPopRealism Abstract: Ink Backgrounds*", ISBN: 978-0615569758 contains teaching projects with step-by-step visual instructions, the drawings' templates, tips, inspirational chapter, much-much more.

FOLLOW UP ACTIVITIES:

View Nadia Russ' NeoPopRealism artwork online and discuss NeoPopRealism ink pen pattern drawing style. Name artists who invented and were top representatives of the new styles of visual arts: Monet - Impressionism, Dali - Surrealism, Picasso - Cubism, Andy Warhol and Jasper Johns - Pop Art, Jeff Koons - Neo-Pop, Nadia Russ - NeoPopRealism.

 Fight bullying in schools to live with dignity with help of NeoPopRealism philosophy and 10 canons for happier life - see www.nadiaruss.com/

Art Lesson Plan 10

GOP (Grand Old Party) - Republican Party's Mascot, the NeoPopRealism Ink Pen / Pattern Drawing

GRADES: 9-12, adapt. 3-5 and 6-8
TIME: Two 45-minute class periods
CONNECTIONS: Visual Arts, History & Politics - Presidential Election
KEY TERMS: NeoPopRealism, Libertarian, liberties, freedom, conservative, election, GOP, Grand Old Party.

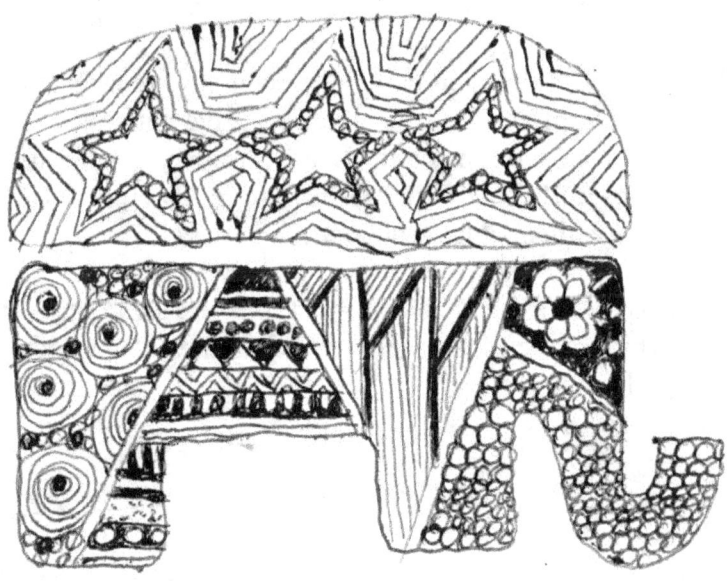

OBJECTIVES:
Students will

- examine Nadia Russ, the NeoPopRealism creator's ink and pen pattern drawings to explore in depth the NeoPopRealism art style and its drawing concept, created in 1989, see page 101 and http://neopoprealismblackwhiteink.blogspot.com/. Compare NeoPopRealism drawings with realist drawings by Rembrandt.
- focus on the politics/ election and how important it is because in 2008-2012, the U.S. changed its direction and went socialistic, which means increasing number of the government workers, less

opportunities for the regular people to achieve the American dream, less freedom and liberties. Remind about struggle of the regular people in the socialist countries such as ex-USSR and Cuba, Cuba is still under the totalitarian regime.
- learn about GOP - Republican Party that promotes freedom and liberty, learn about its logo.
- create GOP's logo in the NeoPopRealist ink and pen / pattern drawing manner.

MATERIALS:
- Computer to see images of the traditional GOP logos, and to see the Nadia Russ' and Rembrandt's drawings online.
- Two Sheets of White Paper 8.5" x 11"
- Ink pen black 0.7 mm

LESSON PLAN ACTIVITIES:
Day 1.
Instruct students about NeoPopRealism ink pen pattern drawing and Nadia Russ, who created this style in 1989 (see page 101 and http://neopoprealismblackwhiteink.blogspot.com/). Have students explore Nadia Russ' NeoPopRealist drawings (purchase posters, see Resources) and drawing by Rembrandt and respond to questions and make comparisons.

Introduce students NeoPopRealism ink pen pattern drawing style/concept: a line creates sections. Then, these sections filled with different imaginative repetitive patterns, some sections left blank. Eraser never used because if a 'mistake' made it visually disappears after the new patterns balance the whole composition (see page 101 and BACKGROUND AND HISTORICAL INFORMATION and http://neopoprealismblackwhiteink.blogspot.com/).

Discuss the GOP's logo executed in the NeoPopRealist manner, using black ink pen. Focus on the repetitive patterns: stars, whirles, circles, zigzags, paralleled lines, strips, etc., ask students to create different patterns on white sheet of paper:

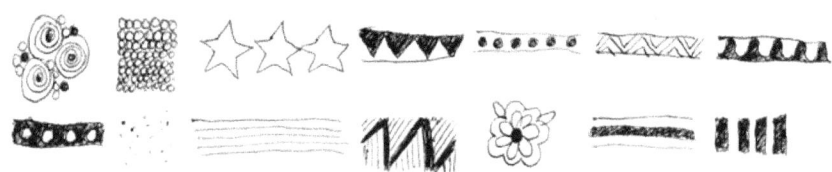

Repetitive patterns used in GOP's mascot

Day 2.
Start 2nd day with a brief discussion of election 2012 and the GOP's history:
Before the general election can be held in November 2012 for the presidency, each of the two major political parties - Republican (GOP) and Democratic - select its nominee through a series of primary elections. To win the nomination, a candidate must amass 50% plus one of delegates' votes.
Republican Mitt Romney accepted the nomination at the Republican National Convention August

27-30 in Tampa, FL. Mitt Romney is a businessman and the former governor of Massachusetts. As governor of Massachusetts, he pushed for a major healthcare reform bill that provided nearly universal coverage. Presidential election was November 6, 2012. Democrats won this election
See GOP's history below.
Remind students NeoPopRealism ink pen / pattern drawing concept (see page 101). Have students draw a GOP logo NeoPopRealism-style using ink pen 0.7 mm.

Have them describe their logos using their knowledge of the GOP's history they recently learned.

ASSESSMENT:
To evaluate NeoPopRealism-style GOP's logo, ask:

- Did the student use the line and several repetitive patterns in the log?

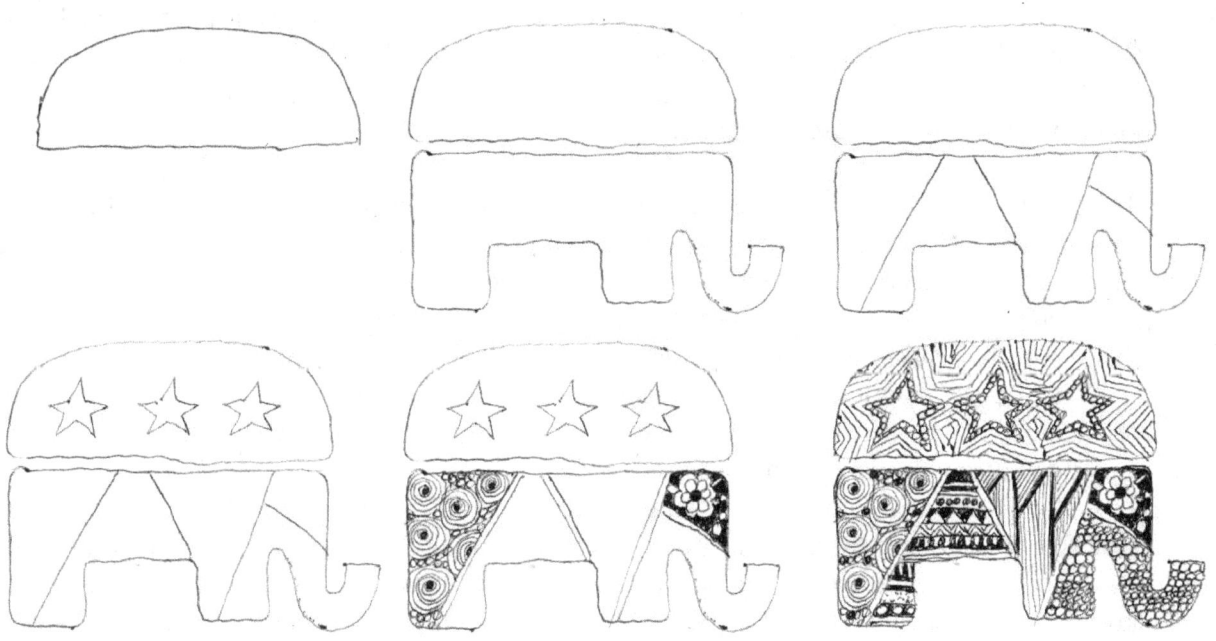

Step-by-step visual instruction

- Write the three words on the back of a sheet of paper with logo-drawing, explaining what the GOP represents. These words must be supported by evidence from the history of GOP.

LESSON PLAN - BACKGROUND and HISTORICAL INFORMATION:
Nadia RUSS is a Ukrainian-born Russian painter/ graphic artist living in the USA, who created a style of visual arts NeoPopRealism. She is famous for innovative NeoPopRealism art and ink pen pattern drawing, including abstract, the meditative style that she created in 1989. Instead of careful copying reality - wild life or human figure, Nadia RUSS creates her artwork using imagination. As

Nadia RUSS experimented and developed her distinctive techniques, her drawings became more symbolic. For her drawings she uses white paper and black ink pen. However, sometimes, she uses blue ink on white paper and gold/silver ink on black paper - http://neopoprealismblackwhiteink.blogspot.com/.

How did Nadia RUSS develop her unique and original style NeoPopRealism? RUSS had studied classical drawing and composition since she was a child, but as she studied she found herself drawn to produce less realistic, more imaginative artwork. In 1989, she created NeoPopRealism art style and ink pattern drawing concept: line creates sections; then, these section filled with different repetitive patterns, some section should be left blank. If artwork made on canvas using color paints and a brush, then, it would be a combination of sections filled with hot and cold color paint, partly with patterns. In 1990, RUSS exhibited her first ink/ pattern drawings in a group exhibition in Moscow's famous Manege. Later, she was exhibiting her artwork in art galleries. In 1996, she moved to the Freeport, Bahamas, where her artwork gained special brightness. In 2000, she came to the USA where she lives till present. Nadia Russ create a term "NeoPopRealism" January 4, 2003. Same year, she manifested her new style of visual arts NeoPopRealism internationally. In 2004, she created NeoPopRealism 10 canons for happier life. In 2006-2007, several US and European museums collected Nadia Russ' paintings and drawings and now, these artworks are in the permanent collections of these museums.

ABOUT REPUBLICAN PARTY. The Republican Party (also called the GOP, for "Grand Old Party") is one of the two major contemporary political parties in the U.S., along with the Democratic Party. 18 presidents have been Republicans. Founded by anti-slavery activists in 1854, it dominated politics nationally for most of the period 1860-1932.

Currently the party's platform generally reflects American conservatism in the U.S. political spectrum. The Republican Party's conservatism is largely based upon its support of classical principles against the modern liberalism of the Democratic Party that is considered American liberalism in contemporary American political discourse.

Founded in the Northern states by anti-slavery activists, modernizers, ex-Whigs and ex-Free Soilers, the Republican Party became the principal opposition to the dominant Souther Democratic Party and the briefly popular Know Nothing Party. The main cause was opposition to the Kansas–Nebraska Act, which repealed the Missouri Compromise by which slavery was kept out of Kansas. The Northern Republicans saw the expansion of slavery as a great evil.

The first public meeting where the name "Republican" was suggested for a new anti-slavery party was held on March 20, 1854 in a schoolhouse in Ripon, Wisconsin.

The first official party convention was held on July 6, 1854 in Jackson, Michigan. By 1858, the Republicans dominated nearly all Northern states. The Republican Party first came to power in 1860 with the election of Abraham Lincoln to the Presidency and Republicans in control of Congress and again, the Northern states. It oversaw the saving of the union, the end of slavery, and the provision of equal rights to all men in the American Civil War and Reconstruction, 1861-1877.

The Republicans' initial base was in the Northeast and the upper Midwest. With the realignment of parties and voters in the Third Party System, the strong run of John C. Fremont in the 1856 Presidential election demonstrated it dominated most northern states.

Early Republican ideology was reflected in the 1856 slogan "free labor, free land, free men", which had been coined by Salmon P. Chase, a Senator from Ohio (and future Secretary of the Treasury and Chief Justice of the U.S.)

"Free labor" referred to the Republican opposition to slave labor and belief in independent artisans and businessmen.

"Free land" referred to Republican opposition to plantation system whereby the rich could buy up all the good farm land and work it with slaves, leaving the yeoman independent farmers the leftovers.

The GOP supported business generally, hard money (i.e., the gold standard), high tariffs to promote economic growth, high wages and high profits, generous pensions for Union veterans, and (after 1893) the annexation of Hawaii. As the northern post-bellum economy boomed with heavy and light industry, railroads, mines, fast-growing cities and prosperous agriculture, the Republicans took credit and promoted policies to sustain the fast growth.

Nevertheless, by 1890 the Republicans had agreed to the Sherman Antitrust Act and the Interstate Commerce Commission in response to complaints from owners of small businesses and farmers. The high McKinley Tariff of 1890 hurt the party and the Democrats swept to a landslide in the off-year elections, even defeating McKinley himself.

After the two terms of Democrat Grover Cleveland, the election of William McKinley in 1896 is widely seen as a resurgence of Republican dominance and is sometimes cited as a realigning election. McKinley promised that high tariffs would end the severe hardship caused by the Panic of 1893, and that the GOP would guarantee a sort of pluralism in which all groups would benefit.

The Republicans were cemented as the party of business, though mitigated by the succession of Theodore Roosevelt who embraced trust busting. He later ran on a third party ticket of the Progressive Party and challenged his previous successor William Howard Taft. The party controlled

the presidency throughout the 1920s, running on a platform of opposition to the League of Nations, high tariffs, and promotion of business interests.

The New Deal coalition of Democrat Franklin D. Roosevelt controlled American politics for most of the next three decades, excepting the two-term presidency of Republican Dwight D. Eisenhower. African Americans moved into the Democratic Party during Roosevelt's time. After Roosevelt took office in 1933, New Deal legislation sailed through Congress at lightning speed. In the 1934 midterm elections, 10 Republican senators went down to defeat, leaving them with only 25 against 71 Democrats. The House of Representatives was split in a similar ratio.

Republicans in Congress heavily criticized the "Second New Deal" and likened it to class warfare and socialism. The volume of legislation, and the inability of the Republicans to block it, soon elevated the level of opposition to Roosevelt. Conservative Democrats, mostly from the South, joined with Republicans led by Senator Robert Taft to create the conservative coalition, which dominated domestic issues in Congress until 1964. The Republicans recaptured Congress in 1946 after gaining 13 seats in the Senate and 55 seats in the House.

The second half of the 20th century saw election or succession of Republican presidents Dwight D. Eisenhower, Richard Nixon, Gerald Ford, Ronald Reagan, George H. W. Bush and George W. Bush.

In the Presidential election of 2008, the party's nominees were Senator John McCain, of Arizona, for President and Alaska Governor Sarah Palin for Vice President. They were defeated by Senator Barack Obama of Illinois and Senator Joe Biden of Delaware.

2010 was a year of political success for the GOP, starting with the upset win of Scott Brown in the Massachusetts special Senate election for the seat held for many decades by the Kennedy brothers. In the November elections, the GOP recaptured control of the House, increased their number of seats in the Senate, and gained a majority of governorships. Additionally, Republicans took control of at least 19 Democratic-controlled state legislatures.

The party's founding members chose the name "Republican Party" in the mid-1850s as homage to the values of republicanism promoted by Thomas Jefferson's Republican party. The idea for the name came from an editorial by the party's leading publicist Horace Greeley, who called for, "some simple name like 'Republican' [that] would more fitly designate those who had united to restore the Union to its true mission of champion and promulgator of Liberty rather than propagandist of slavery." The name reflects the 1776 republican values of civic virtue and opposition to aristocracy and corruption.

The term "Grand Old Party" (GOP) is a traditional nickname for the Republican Party. The term originated in 1875 in the Congressional Record, referring to the party associated with the successful military defense of the Union as "this gallant old party"; the following year in an article in the Cincinnati Commercial, the term was modified to "grand old party". The first use of the abbreviation is dated 1884.

The traditional mascot of the party is the elephant. A political cartoon by Thomas Nast, published in Harper's Weekly on November 7, 1874, is considered the first important use of the symbol. In the early 20th century, the usual symbol of the Republican Party in Midwestern states such as Indiana and Ohio was the bald eagle, as opposed to the Democratic rooster.

After the 2000 election, the color red became associated with the GOP, although the party has not officially adopted it.

The Republican Party includes fiscal conservatives, social conservatives, neoconservatives, moderates, and libertarians. Republicans emphasize the role of free markets and individual achievement as the primary factors behind economic prosperity. To this end, they favor laissez-faire economics, fiscal conservatism, and the promotion of personal responsibility over welfare programs.

Most Republicans agree there should be a "safety net" to assist the less fortunate; however, they tend to believe the private sector is more effective in helping the poor than government is. As a result, Republicans support giving government grants to faith-based and other private charitable organizations to supplant welfare spending.

Many contemporary Republicans voice support of strict constructionism, the judicial philosophy that the Constitution should be interpreted narrowly and as close to the original intent as is practicable rather than a more flexible "living Constitution" model.

Most Republicans support school choice through charter schools and school vouchers for private schools; many have denounced the performance of the public school system and the teachers' unions. The party has insisted on a system of greater accountability for public schools, most prominently in recent years with the No Child Left Behind Act of 2001.

The Republican Party has always advocated a strong national defense, historically they disapproved
of interventionist foreign policy actions.

The GOP is usually seen as the traditionally pro-business party and it garners major support from a wide variety of industries from the financial sector to small businesses. Republicans are about 50 percent more likely to be self-employed, and are more likely to work in management.

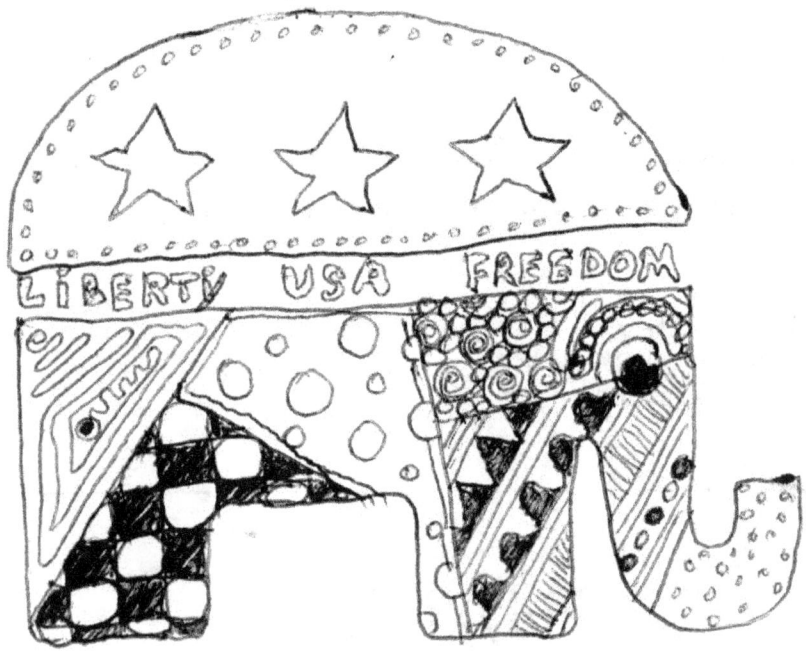

RESOURCES:

1. Information on NeoPopRealism ink pen/ pattern drawing, its concept and Nadia Russ biography, who created this style in 1989: page 101 and http://neopoprealismblackwhiteink.blogspot.com/

2. Wall decals with NeoPopRealism ink pen drawings at 33% off for educators: www.neopoprealism.net

3. A book "*How to Draw NeoPopRealism Ink Images: Basics*", ISBN: 978-0615515755 includes a few teaching projects with step-by-step drawing instructions and all you need to know to learn how to draw NeoPopRealism.

FOLLOW UP ACTIVITIES:
Discuss NeoPopRealism ink pen pattern drawing style. Name artists who invented new styles of visual arts and were the best representatives: Monet - Impressionism, Dali - Surrealism, Picasso - Cubism, Andy Warhol and Jasper Johns - Pop Art, Jeff Koons - Neo-Pop, Nadia Russ - NeoPopRealism.

Ask students questions about GOP history and its logo.
Fight bullying in school with help of NeoPopRealism philosophy and its 10 canons for happier life.

Art lesson plan 11

Humorous Thanksgiving Greeting Card "Never Give Up!" - NeoPopRalism/ NeoWhimsy Ink Pen / Pattern Drawing Style

GRADES: 6-8, adapt. 3-5, 9-12
SUBJECT: Visual arts, technology, music
TIME: Two 45-minute class periods

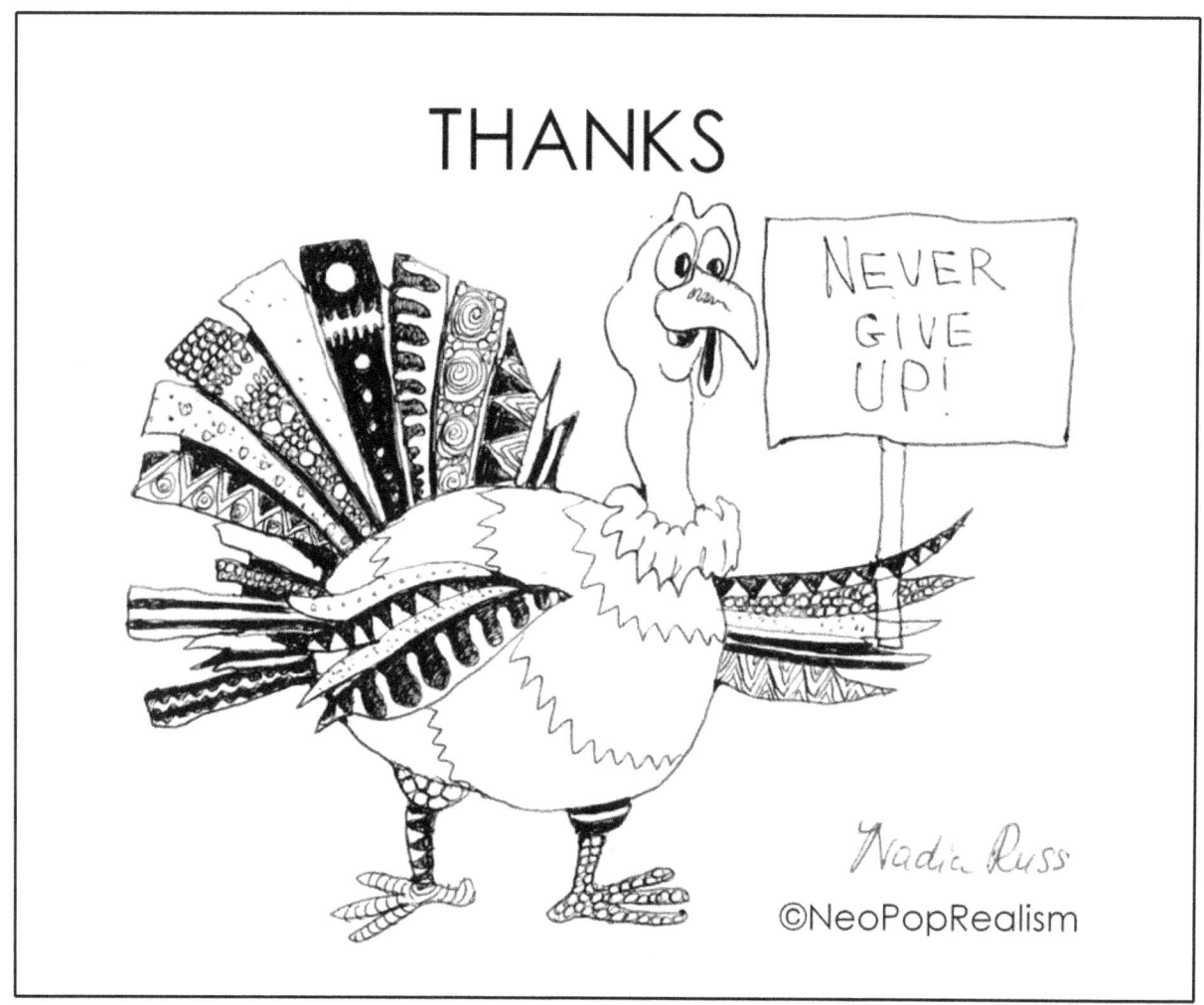

OBJECTIVES:
Students will
- learn about Thanksgiving and its history;
- explore the NeoPopRealism ink pen / pattern drawing style created by artist Nadia Russ n 1989 and NeoWhimsies, the simplified NeoPopRealism ink pen pattern drawings - NeoWhimsies are the simplified NeoPopRealism ink pen / pattern drawings;
- create a unique greeting card using a theme 'Thanksgiving Thank You';
- focus/ model: Greeting Cards
- print copies from the student's greeting cards *"Never Give Up!"* that they drew during the art lesson. Students can send these cards or give on Thanksgiving day to their friends and relatives.

VOCABULARY:
NeoPopRealism, NeoWhimsy, Card, Layout, Text, Image, Fold, Postage

MATERIALS:
- Two sheets of white thick paper - cardstock - size 8.5"x11"
- Black ink pen thin 0.7 mm.
- Computer
- Printer

LESSON ACTIVITIES:

Day 1.
Class Period One:
Tell students a brief history of Thanksgiving (see page 54)
Examine the NeoPopRealism-NeoWhimsy greeting card *"Never Give Up!"*.

Instruct students about NeoPopRealism ink pen / pattern drawing style, its concept, and Nadia Russ, who created this art style in 1989 (see page 101, "LESSON PLAN BACKGROUND and HISTORICAL INFORMATION" and in http://neopoprealismblackwhiteink.blogspot.com/).
Examine the traditional-realistic drawings of the turkey (find them online or use photographs/ prints). Have students respond to questions and make comparisons how the NeoPopRealist image of turkey is different from the traditional-realistic images of turkey, emphasizing use of ink pen, lines and patterns, contrasting and flatness to convey the character and emotion.

Discuss turkey - where the turkeys live, the bird's body proportions, tail, wings, head, the character of this bird. A turkey is a large bird in the genus Meleagris. Meleagris gallopavo, commonly known as the Wild Turkey, is native to the forests of North America. The domestic turkey is a descendant of this species. The other living species is Meleagris ocellata or the Ocellated Turkey, native to the forests of the Yucatán Peninsula. Turkeys are classed in the taxonomic order of Galliformes. Within this order they are relatives of the grouse family or subfamily. Males of both species have a distinctive fleshy wattle or protuberance that hangs from the top of the beak—called a snood in the Wild Turkey and its domestic descendants. They are among the largest birds in their ranges. As in many galliform species, the male (tom or gobbler) is larger and much more colorful than the female (hen).

Focus on the repetitive patterns used in NeoPopRealist drawing of a greeting card *"Never Give Up!"*, ask students to reproduce these patterns and create new ones, all on separate white sheet of paper using ink pen 0.7 mm (see illustration) - the strips, zigzags, waves, circles, whirles, dots, their variations and combinations.

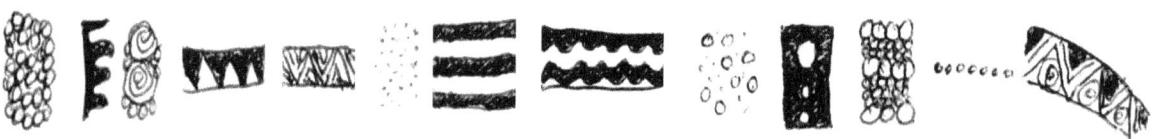

Patterns used in greeting card "Never Give Up!"

Day 2.
Class Period Two:
Remind students the NeoPopRealism ink pen/ pattern drawing concept (see LESSON PLAN BACKGROUND and HISTORICAL INFORMATION): a line creates a form, then this form divided into sections, then sections filled with different repetitive patterns.
Have students fold a sheet of paper 8.5"x11" at the middle, do not cut it. Have students turn it horizontal - the folding line must be on the top. Students draw the image of greeting card *"Never Give Up!"* - a contour of a turkey on the middle. Have students draw the turkey's tail and the wings, it will create the sections. Then, they fill these sections with different repetitive patterns. Some section should be left blank. Students create the NeoPopRealist Greeting card *"Never Give Up!"* using their new knowledge related to NeoPopRealism and imagination. Encourage them to use imagination and create the new patterns instead of copying the offered ones.

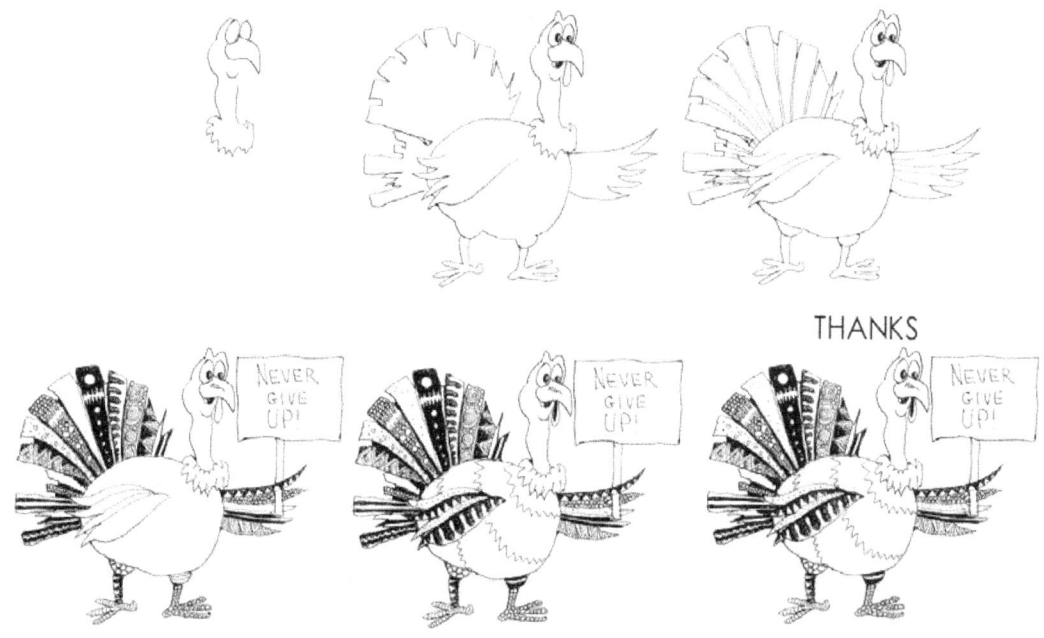

Have students discuss why they included each element-pattern, and what was difficult and easy while creating a NeoPopRealist Greeting card *"Never Give Up!"* Have them describe the meaning of this card and the expression *"Never Give Up!"*. Suggest print at home or print in school, using printer, the cards from the students' recently made the NeoPopRealism *"Never Give Up!"* greeting cards. Suggest to send or give these cards to the relatives or friends on Thanksgiving day.

EVALUATION:
Did the student show an understanding of the artistic concept of NeoPopRealism and NeoWhimsies?
Did the student follow directions and the guidelines?
Did the student create a piece of art of a greeting card *"Never Give Up!"* in NeoPopRalism ink pen / pattern drawing style - image NeoWhimsy turkey?

ESOL STRATEGIES:
Cooperative learning, learning of new material, activating background knowledge, music, total physical response, communication, multi-sensory approach, direct instruction.

ART LESSSON PLAN BACKGROUND and HISTORICAL INFORMATION:
Nadia Russ and NeoPopRealism:
Nadia RUSS is a Ukrainian-born Russian painter/ graphic artist living in the USA, who created a style of visual arts NeoPopRealism http://neopoprealismblackwhiteink.blogspot.com . She is famous for innovative NeoPopRealism art and ink pen pattern drawing, including abstract, the meditative style that she created in 1989. Instead of careful copying reality - wild life or human figure, Nadia RUSS creates her artwork using imagination. As Nadia RUSS experimented and developed her distinctive techniques, her drawings became more symbolic. For her drawings she uses white paper and black ink pen. However, sometimes, she uses blue ink on white paper and gold/silver ink on black paper. See http://neopoprealismblackwhiteink.blogspot.com.

How did Nadia RUSS develop her unique and original style NeoPopRealism? RUSS had studied classical drawing and composition since she was a child, but as she studied she found herself drawn to produce less realistic, more imaginative artwork. In 1989, she created NeoPopRealism art style and ink pattern drawing concept: line creates sections; then, these section filled with different repetitive patterns, some section should be left blank. If artwork made on canvas using color paints and a brush, then, it would be a combination of sections filled with hot and cold color paint, partly with patterns. In 1990, RUSS exhibited her first ink/ pattern drawings in a group exhibition in Moscow's famous Manege. Later, she was exhibiting her artwork in art galleries. In 1996, she moved to the Freeport, Bahamas, where her artwork gained special brightness. In 2000, she came to the USA where she lives till present. Nadia Russ create a term "NeoPopRealism" January 4, 2003. Same year, she manifested her new style of visual arts NeoPopRealism internationally. In 2004, she created NeoPopRealism 10 canons for happier life. In 2006-2007, several US and European museums collected Nadia Russ' paintings and drawings and now, these artworks are in the permanent collections of these museums.

ABOUT THANKSGIVING DAY.

Thanksgiving Day is a holiday celebrated primarily in the USA Canada. Thanksgiving is celebrated on the fourth Thursday of November in the United States and on the second Monday of October in Canada. The celebration often extends to the weekend that falls closest to the day it is celebrated. Several other places around the world have similar celebrations. Historically, Thanksgiving had roots in religious and cultural tradition. Today, Thanksgiving is primarily celebrated as a secular holiday.

The holiday's history in North America is rooted in English traditions dating from the Protestant Reformation. In the United States, the modern Thanksgiving holiday tradition is commonly traced to a 1621 celebration at Plymouth in present-day Massachusetts. The 1621 Plymouth feast and thanksgiving was prompted by a good harvest. In later years, the tradition was continued by civil leaders such as Governor Bradford who planned a thanksgiving celebration and fast in 1623. The practice of holding an annual harvest festival like this did not become a regular affair in New England until the late 1660s. Pilgrims and Puritans who began emigrating from England in the 1620s and 1630s carried the tradition of Days of Fasting and Days of Thanksgiving with them to New England. Several days of Thanksgiving were held in early New England history that have been identified as the "First Thanksgiving", including Pilgrim holidays in Plymouth in 1621 and 1623, and a Puritan holiday in Boston in 1631. Thanksgiving proclamations were made mostly by church leaders in New England up until 1682, and then by both state and church leaders until after the American Revolution. During the revolutionary period, political influences affected the issuance of Thanksgiving proclamations. Various proclamations were made by royal governors, John Hancock, General George Washington, and the Continental Congress, each giving thanks to God for events favorable to their causes. As President of the United States, George Washington proclaimed the first nation-wide thanksgiving celebration in America marking November 26, 1789, "as a day of public thanksgiving and prayer to be observed by acknowledging with grateful hearts the many and signal favours of Almighty God". According to historian Jeremy Bangs, director of the Leiden American Pilgrim Museum, the Pilgrims may have been influenced by watching the annual services of Thanksgiving for the relief of the siege of Leiden in 1574, while they were staying in Leiden. Every year, the President of the United States will "pardon" a turkey, which spares the bird's life and ensures that it will spend the duration of its life roaming freely on farmland.

RESOURCES:

1. Information on NeoPopRealism ink pen/ pattern drawing, its concept and Nadia Russ, who created this style in 1989: page 101 and http://neopoprealismblackwhiteink.blogspot.com/

2. Wall decals with NeoPopRealism ink pen drawings at 33% off for educators: www.neopoprealism.net

3. A book "*How to Draw Advanced NeoPopRealism Ink Images*", ISBN: 978-0615569758. It contains a few teaching projects with step-by-step images and patterns drawing instructions, more.

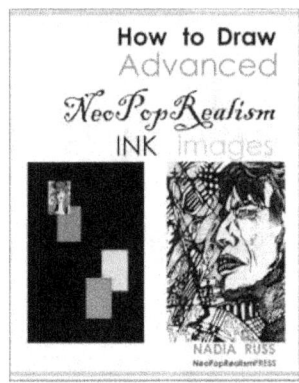

4. Photographs or prints with the realistic drawings of turkey to compare.

FOLLOW UP ACTIVITIES:
View Nadia Russ' NeoPopRealism artwork online and discuss NeoPopRealism ink pen pattern drawing style. Name the artists who invented new styles of visual arts and were their best representatives: Monet - Impressionism, Dali - Surrealism, Picasso - Cubism, Andy Warhol and Jasper Johns - Pop Art, Jeff Koons - Neo-Pop, Nadia Russ - NeoPopRealism.

Fight bullying in schools to live with dignity with help of NeoPopRealism philosophy and 10 canons
for happier life - see page 101 and www.nadiaruss.com/.

Art Lesson Plan 12

A Carnival's Pony, Inspired by Nadia Russ & NeoPopRealism Ink Pen / Pattern Drawing

GRADES: 9-12, adapt 3-5, 6-8
SUBJECT: Visual Arts & Music, Equine Art

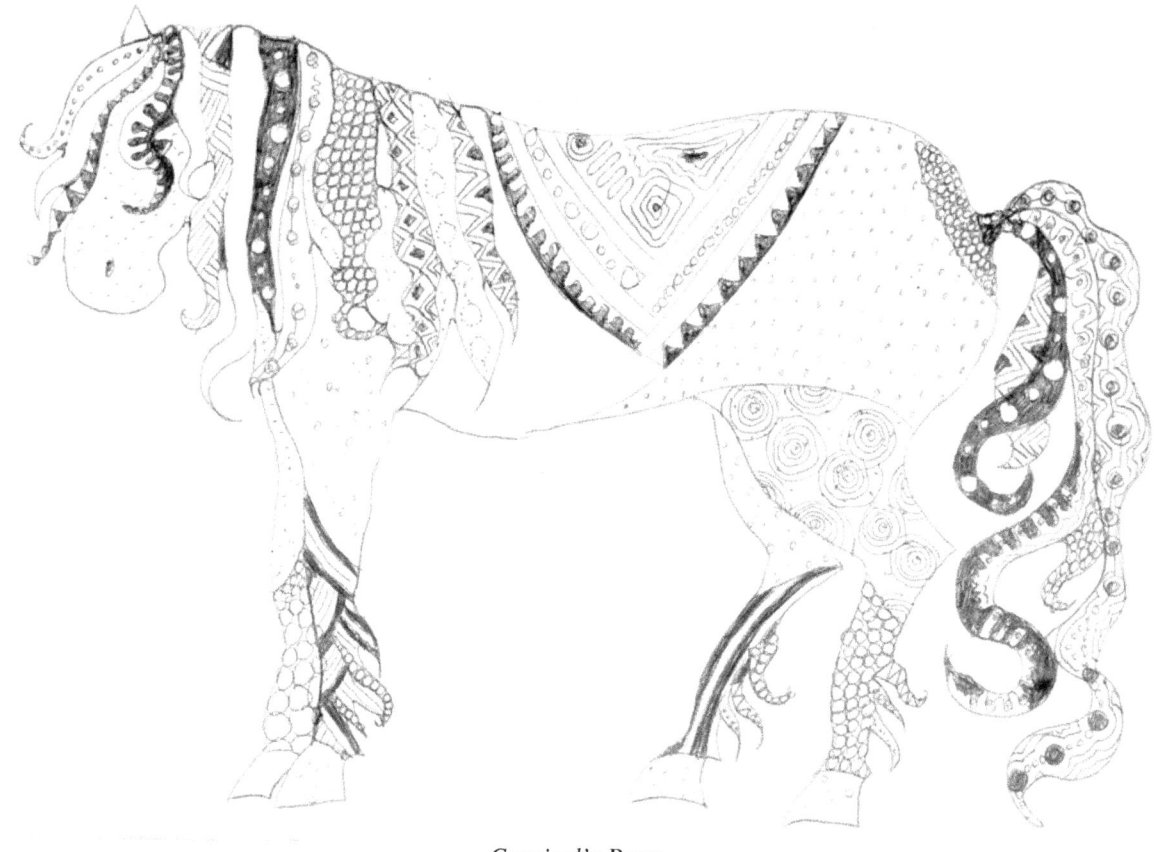

Carnival's Pony

OBJECTIVES
:Students will
- explore NeoPopRealism ink pen pattern drawing and work of artist Nadia Russ who created this

style in 1989 (see page 101);
- define the term "NeoPopRealism"
- differentiate NeoPopRealism drawing from realism approach.
- Experiment with drawing the repetitive patterns.
- create a Carnival's Pony inspired by the drawings by Nadia Russ using ink pen and white paper, without preparation and without eraser (important).

MATERIAL:
- ink pen black 0.7mm
- 8.5"x11" white papers (2)

LESOON PLAN ACTIVITIES:

Day 1:
Display in classroom posters with Nadia Russ' NeoPopRealism ink pen pattern drawings (see RESOURCES). Introduce (or remind about) the NeoPopRealism ink pen pattern drawing concept and artist Nadia Russ biography, who created this style in 1989, see page 101 and http://neopoprealismblackwhiteink.blogspot.com/. Ask students to compare drawings by Nadia Russ and drawings by old master such as Rembrandt.

Show students several pictures of ponies. Discuss with students the ponies, their special and unique characteristics and importance. Ponies are generally considered intelligent and friendly, sometimes they also are described as stubborn or cunning. Discuss about how pony can be trained and used in carnivals. Notice such things as the shape and position of the head, legs, tail, and so on.

Examine closely the NeoPopRealist Carnival's Pony drawing (see illustration) and then ask students the following questions:
- What words would they use to describe the pony in this artwork?
- Did the artist look at a real pony or use imagination to create this work? What makes you think this way?
- What is most interesting about this artwork?
- What do you think the artist is trying to say about pony? What makes you think this?

Prepare ink pen and paper for all students.
Each student will draw a *Carnival's Pony*. Demonstrate the drawing of a *Carnival's Pony*. Using a line, create a pony's shape. Then, divide it asymmetrically into sections. Then, fill sections with different repetitive patterns: circles, dots, whirles, lines, zigzags, more. Some sections leave blank. Explain (or remind) why NeoPopRealism ink pattern drawing needs no eraser: if a 'mistake' made, it visually disappears because the following patterns make this 'mistake' invisible and the whole composition balanced. Explain contrast and flatness of the NeoPopRealism ink pen pattern drawing.

Offer students sheets of 8.5"x11" paper, divided into squares/section and turn on music (not loud, preferable jazz). Offer students create in each section/square different repetitive patterns using imagination. Drawing patterns is meditative process. Students can finish drawing the patterns at home.

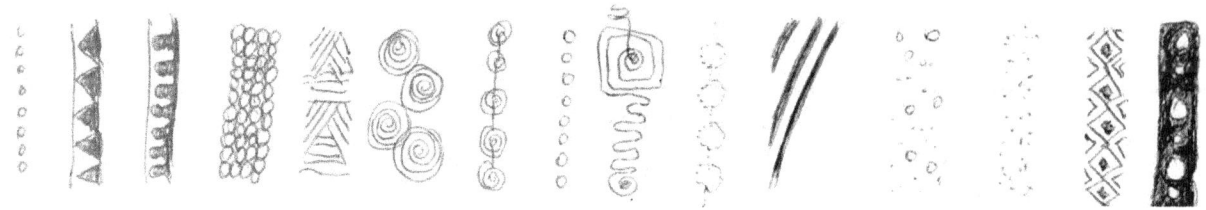

The patterns used in drawing Carnival's Pony

Day 2:

Remind students the NeoPopRealism ink pen/ pattern drawing concept: a line creates sections, then these sections filled with different repetitive patterns, some sections left blank. Eraser never used. Turn on music (not loud). Students draw a shape of a *Carnival Pony*. Then, they divide a pony's shape into sections and fill each section with different pattern, some section(s) should be left blank. When work is finished, students title and sign their artworks. The students compare their drawings and discuss the NeoPopRealism ink pen / pattern drawing concept and patterns they used in

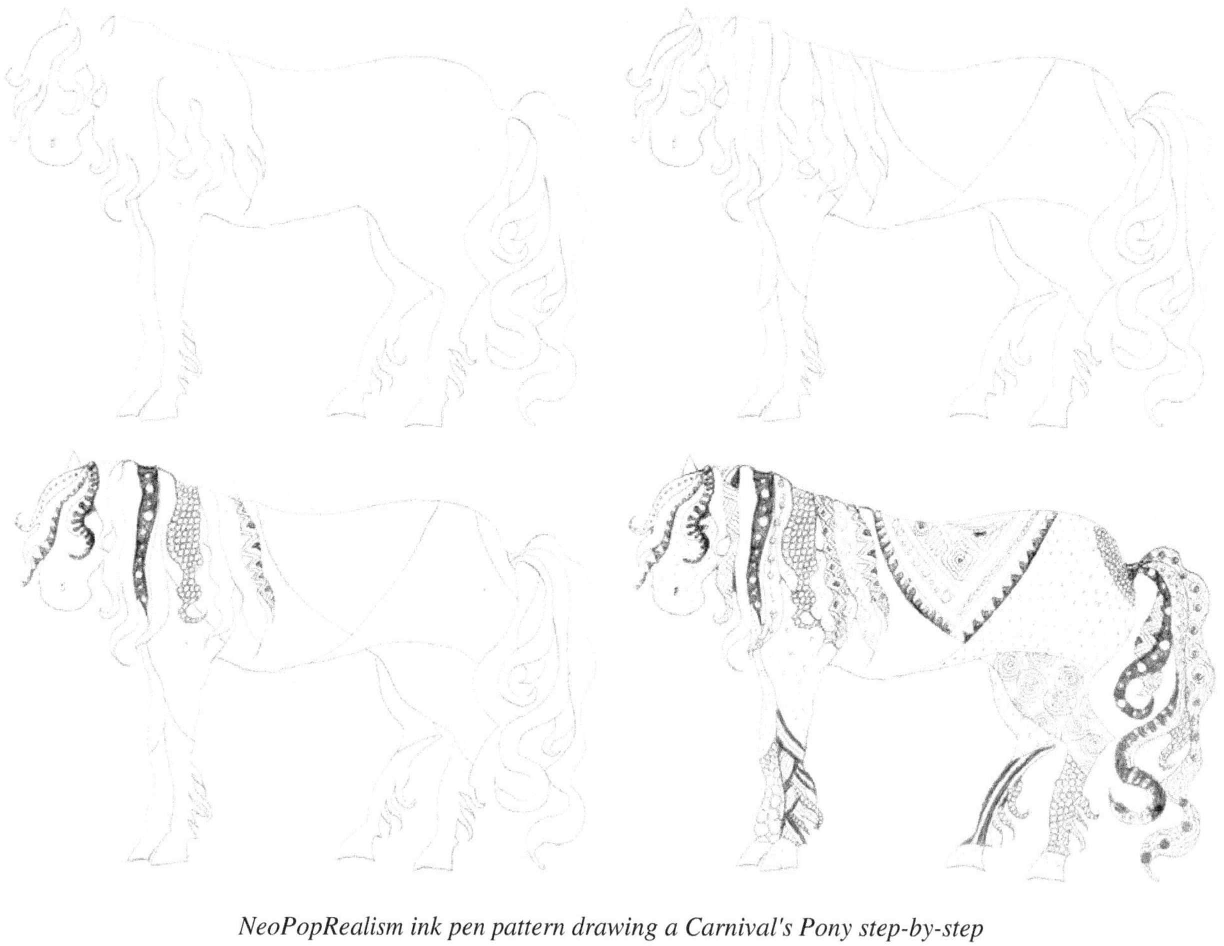

NeoPopRealism ink pen pattern drawing a Carnival's Pony step-by-step

drawings. Ask what was difficult/easy and what they will do different next time. Students define a terms "NeoPopRealism."

Briefly introduce students the Pony Club that exist in over 30 countries worldwide; ages of participants range from eight to twenty-five. See more information in LESSON BACKGROUND and HISTORICAL INFORMATIN and in http://www.ponyclub.org/.

LESSON PLAN BACKGROUND and HISTORICAL INFORMATION:

Nadia RUSS is a Ukrainian-born Russian painter/ graphic artist living in the USA, who created a style of visual arts NeoPopRealism. She is famous for innovative NeoPopRealism art and ink pen pattern drawing, including abstract, the meditative style that she created in 1989. Instead of careful copying reality - wild life or human figure, Nadia RUSS creates her artwork using imagination. As Nadia RUSS experimented and developed her distinctive techniques, her drawings became more symbolic. For her drawings she uses white paper and black ink pen. However, sometimes, she uses blue ink on white paper and gold/silver ink on black paper. http://neopoprealismblackwhiteink.blogspot.com/

How did Nadia RUSS develop her unique and original style NeoPopRealism? RUSS had studied classical drawing and composition since she was a child, but as she studied she found herself drawn to produce less realistic, more imaginative artwork. In 1989, she created NeoPopRealism art style and ink pattern drawing concept: a line creates sections; then, these section filled with different repetitive patterns, some section left blank. If artwork made on canvas using color paints and a brush, then, it would be a combination of sections filled with hot and cold color paint, partly with patterns. In 1990, RUSS exhibited her first ink/ pattern drawings in a group exhibition in Moscow's famous Manege. Later, she was exhibiting her artwork in art galleries. In 1996, she moved to the Freeport, Bahamas, where her artwork gained special brightness. In 2000, she came to the USA where she lives till present. Nadia Russ create a term "NeoPopRealism" January 4, 2003. Same year, she manifested her new style of visual arts NeoPopRealism internationally. In 2004, she created NeoPopRealism 10 canons for happier life. In 2006-2007, several US and European museums collected Nadia Russ' paintings and drawings and now, these artworks are in the permanent collections of these museums.

ABOUT PONY. A pony is a small horse (Equus ferus caballus). A pony is a horse that is under an approximate or exact height at the withers, or a small horse with a specific conformation and temperament. There are many different breeds. Compared to other horses, ponies often exhibit thicker manes, tails and overall coat, as well as proportionally shorter legs, wider barrels, heavier bone, thicker necks, and shorter heads with broader foreheads. The word "pony" derives from the old French poulenet, meaning foal, a young, immature horse, but this is not the modern meaning; unlike a horse foal, a pony remains small when fully grown.

The ancestors of most modern ponies developed small stature due to living on the margins of livable horse habitat. These smaller animals were domesticated and bred for various purposes all over the northern hemisphere. Ponies were historically used for driving and freight transport, as children's mounts, for recreational riding, and later as competitors and performers in their own right. During the Industrial Revolution, particularly in Great Britain, a significant number were used as pit ponies, hauling loads of coal in the mines.

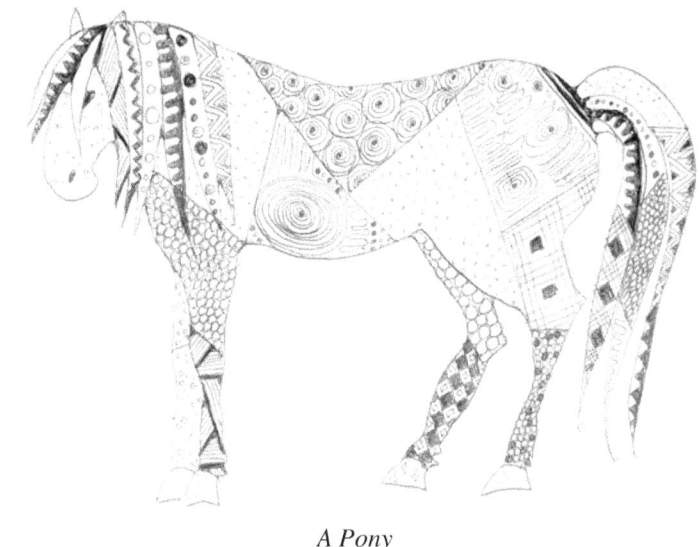

A Pony

Ponies are generally considered intelligent and friendly, though sometimes they also are described as stubborn or cunning. Properly trained ponies are appropriate mounts for children who are learning to ride. Larger ponies can be ridden by adults, as ponies are usually strong for their size. In modern use, many organizations define a pony as a mature horse that measures less than 58 inches, 147 cm at the withers, but there are a number of exceptions. Different organizations that use a strict measurement model vary from 56 inches, 142 cm to 59 inches, 150 cm. Many breeds classify an animal as either horse or pony based on pedigree and phenotype, no matter its height. Some full-sized horses may be called "ponies" for various reasons of tradition or as a term of endearment.

In many parts of the world ponies are used as working animals, as pack animals and for pulling various horse-drawn vehicles. They are used for children's pony rides at traveling carnivals and at children's private parties where small children can take short rides on ponies that are saddled and then either led individually or hitched to a "pony wheel" (a non-motorized device akin to a hot walker) that leads six to eight ponies at a time. Ponies are widely used for pony trekking and other forms of Equitourism riding holidays, often carrying adults as well as children.

Pony Clubs, open to young people who own either horses or ponies, are formed worldwide to educate young people about horses, promote responsible horse ownership, and also sponsor competitive events for young people and smaller horses.

FOLLOW UP ACTIVITIES:
View Nadia Russ artwork online and discuss NeoPopRealism ink pen pattern drawing style. Name artists who invented new styles of visual arts and were best representative: Monet - Impressionism, Dali - Surrealism, Picasso - Cubism, Andy Warhol and Jasper Johns - Pop Art, Jeff Koons - Neo-Pop, Nadia Russ - NeoPopRealism.

RESOURCES:
- Wall decals with NeoPopRealism ink pen drawings at 33% off for educators:
www.neopoprealism.net

- Photographs of ponies to examine this animal more closely.

- Information on NeoPopRealism ink pen/ pattern drawing, its concept and Nadia Russ' biography, who created this style in 1989: see page 101 and http://neopoprealismblackwhiteink.blogspot.com/

Fight bullying in school with NeoPopRealism 10 canons for happier life, see page 101.

Art Lesson Plan 13

Greeting Card "Merry Christmas!" in NeoPopRalism ink pen / pattern drawing style - NeoWhimsy

SUBJECT: Visual arts, music, technology.
GRAGES: 9-12, adapt. 3-5, 6-8
 TIME: Two 45-minute class periods

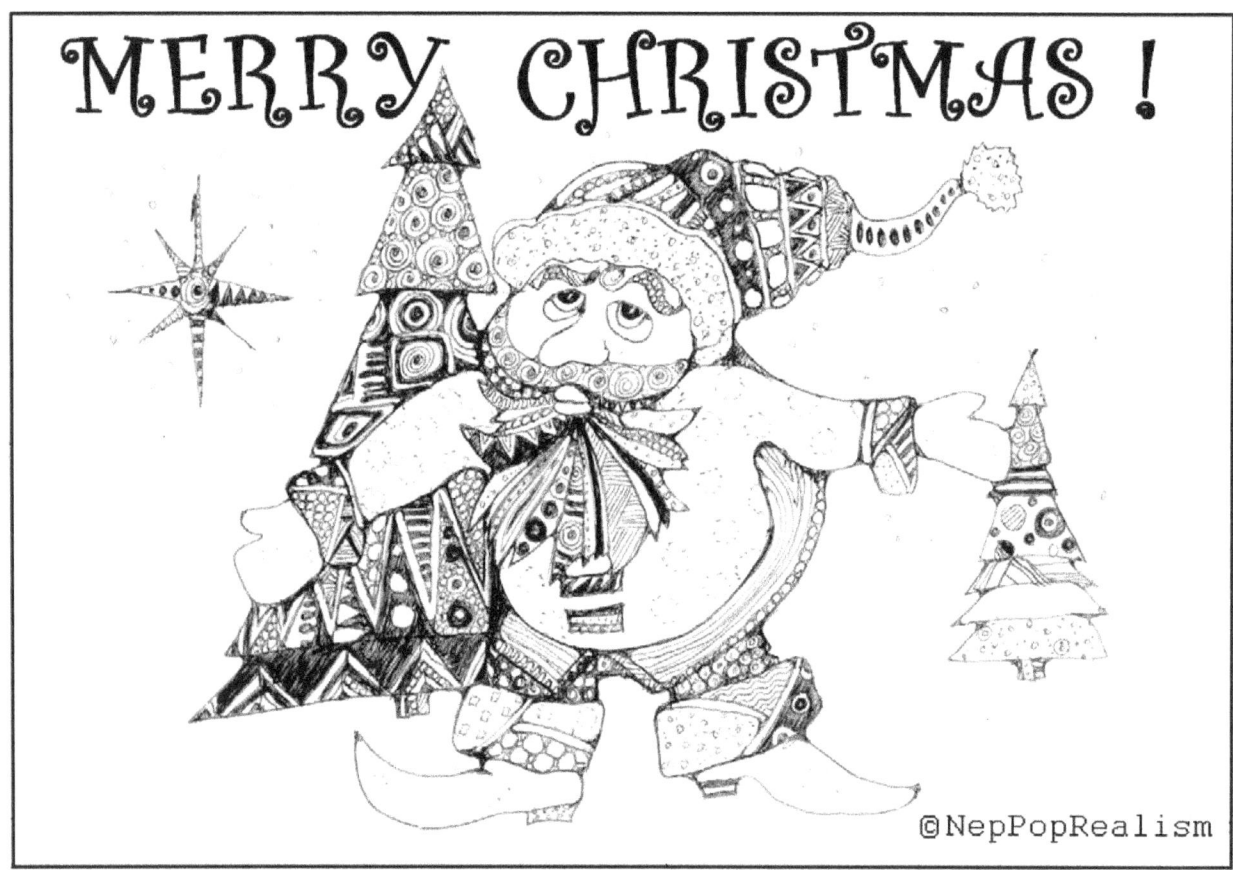

OBJECTIVES
Students will:
- learn about Christmas and its history;
   - explore the NeoPopRealism ink pen / pattern drawing style created by artist Nadia Russ in 1989
   and NeoWhimsies, the simplified NeoPopRealism ink pen / pattern drawings;

- create a unique greeting card's NeoPopRealism ink pen drawings using a theme Christmas;
- focus/ model: Greeting Cards
- print copies from the students' greeting cards *"Merry Christmas!"* they drew during the art lesson. Students send these cards or give for Christmas to friends and relatives.

VOCABULARY: NeoPopRealism, NeoWhimsy, Card, Layout, Text, Image, Fold, Postage, Christmas.

MATERIALS:
- Two sheets of white thick paper - cardstock - size 8.5"x11"
- Black ink pen 0.7 mm.
- Computer
- Printer

Day 1.
Class Period One:
Tell students a brief history of Christmas (see LESSON PLAN BACKGROUND and HISTORICAL INFORMATION).
Examine the NeoPopRealism-NeoWhimsy greeting card *"Merry Christmas!"*.
Instruct students about NeoPopRealism ink pen / pattern drawing style, its concept, and Nadia Russ, who created this art style in 1989, see LESSON PLAN BACKGROUND and HISTORICAL INFORMATION and page 101.
Examine the traditional-realistic drawings of Santa Claus (find them online or use photographs/ prints). Have students respond to questions and make comparisons how the NeoPopRealist image of Santa Claus is different from traditional-realistic images of Santa Claus, emphasizing use of ink pen, lines and patterns, contrasting (black ink on white paper) to convey the character and emotion.

Discuss Christmas day and its history and celebration, see LESSON PLAN BACKGROUND and HISTORICAL INFORMATION .
Discuss Santa Claus, who is a portly, joyous, white-bearded man, regularly wearing a red coat with white collar and cuffs, white-cuffed red trousers, and black leather belt and boots. Images of him rarely have a beard with no moustache. This image popular in the US and Canada since 19th century due to the significant influence of Clement Clarke Moore's 1823 poem "A Visit From St. Nicholas" and of caricaturist and political cartoonist Thomas Nast. This image has been maintained and reinforced through songs, radio, television, children's books and films. See more on Santa Claus and Christmas Day in "Art lesson plan background and historical Information." Focus on the repetitive patterns used in NeoPopRealist ink pen pattern drawing of the greeting card "Merry Christmas!". Ask students to reproduce these patterns and create new ones on separate white sheet of paper, using ink pen 0.7 mm - the strips, zigzags, waves, circles, whirles, dots, their variations and combinations:

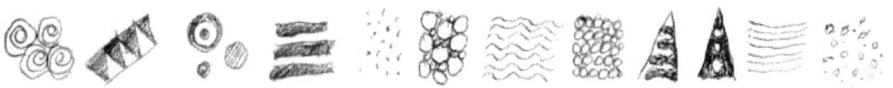

Day 2.

Class Period Two:

Remind students the NeoPopRealism ink pen/ pattern drawing concept (see LESSON PLAN BACKGROUND and HISTORICAL INFORMATION and page 101): a line creates a form, then this form divided into sections, then these sections filled with different repetitive patterns.

Have students fold a sheet of paper 8.5"x11" on the middle, do not cut it.

Have students turn it horizontal - the folding line must be on the top.

Students draw the images of a greeting card *"Merry Christmas!"* - the contours of Santa Claus' body and Christmas trees.

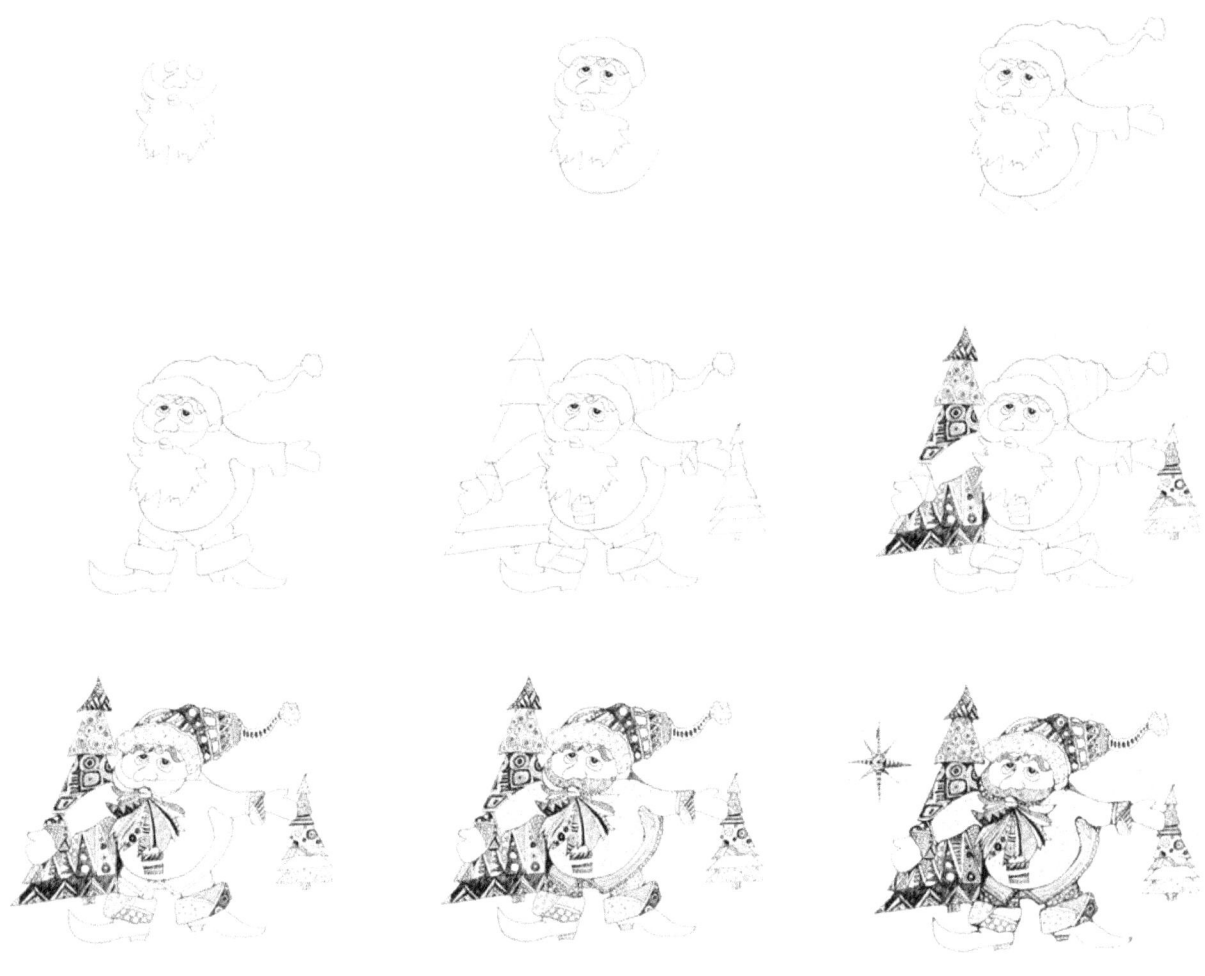

Have students divide the Santa Claus' beard, hat, the trees, and more into sections. Then, they fill these sections with different repetitive patterns, some sections they leave blank. Students create the NeoPopRealist Greeting card *"Merry Christmas*!" using their knowledge about NeoPopRealism ink pen/ pattern drawing. Encourage them to use imagination and create the new patterns instead of copying those they see in a sample greeting card.

Have students discuss why they included each element-pattern and what was difficult and easy

While creating the NeoPopRealist Greeting card *"Merry Christmas!"*
Have them describe the meaning of this card - Christmas Day and Santa Claus.
Suggest students to print at home or print in school, using printer, the several greeting cards from those recently created.
Suggest to send or give those cards to the relatives and friends for Christmas.

EVALUSTION:
Did the students follow directions and the guidelines?
Did the students show an understanding of the artistic concepts of NeoPopRealism and NeoWhimsies?
Did the students create a piece of art of a Greeting Card *"Merry Christmas!"* in NeoPopRalism ink pen / pattern drawing style - image NeoWhimsy Santa Claus?

ESOL Strategies:
Cooperative learning, learning of new material, activating background knowledge, music, total physical response, communication, multi-sensory approach, direct instruction.

ART LESSON PLAN BACKGROUND AND HISTORICAL INFORMATION:
Nadia Russ and NeoPopRealism:
Nadia RUSS is a Ukrainian-born Russian painter/ graphic artist living in the USA, who created a style of visual arts NeoPopRealism http://neopoprealismblackwhiteink.blogspot.com/. She is famous for innovative NeoPopRealism art and ink pen pattern drawing, including abstract, the meditative style that she created in 1989. Instead of careful copying reality - wild life or human figure, Nadia RUSS creates her artwork using imagination. As Nadia RUSS experimented and developed her distinctive techniques, her drawings became more symbolic. For her drawings she uses white paper and black ink pen. However, sometimes, she uses blue ink on white paper and gold/silver ink on black paper - http://neopoprealismblackwhiteink.blogspot.com/.

How did Nadia RUSS develop her unique and original style NeoPopRealism? RUSS had studied classical drawing and composition since she was a child, but as she studied she found herself drawn to produce less realistic, more imaginative artwork. In 1989, she created NeoPopRealism art style and ink pattern drawing concept: line creates sections; then, these section filled with different repetitive patterns, some section should be left blank. If artwork made on canvas using color paints and a brush, then, it would be a combination of sections filled with hot and cold color paint, partly with patterns. In 1990, RUSS exhibited her first ink/ pattern drawings in a group exhibition in Moscow's famous Manege. Later, she was exhibiting her artwork in art galleries. In 1996, she moved to the Freeport, Bahamas, where her artwork gained special brightness. In 2000, she came to the USA where she lives till present. Nadia Russ create a term "NeoPopRealism" January 4, 2003. Same year, she manifested her new style of visual arts NeoPopRealism internationally. In 2004, she created NeoPopRealism 10 canons for happier life. In 2006-2007, several US and European museums collected Nadia Russ' paintings and drawings and now, these artworks are in the permanent collections of these museums.

CHRISTMAS DAY and SANTA CLAUS.

Santa Claus, also known as Saint Nicholas, Father Christmas and simply "Santa", is a figure with legendary, mythical, historical and folkloric origins who, in many western cultures, is said to bring gifts to the homes of the good children during the late evening and overnight hours of Christmas Eve, December 24. The modern figure was derived from the Dutch figure of Sinterklaas, which, in turn, may have part of its basis in hagiographical tales concerning the historical figure of gift giver Saint Nicholas. A nearly identical story is attributed by Greek and Byzantine folklore to Basil of Caesarea. Basil's feast day on January 1 is considered the time of exchanging gifts in Greece. Santa Claus is generally depicted as a portly, joyous, white-bearded man - sometimes with spectacles - wearing a red coat with white collar and cuffs, white-cuffed red trousers, and black leather belt and boots (images of him rarely have a beard with no moustache). This image became popular in the United States and Canada in the 19th century due to the significant influence of Clement Clarke Moore's 1823 poem "A Visit From St. Nicholas" and of caricaturist and political cartoonist Thomas Nast. This image has been maintained and reinforced through song, radio, television, children's books and films.

According to a tradition which can be traced to the 1820s, Santa Claus lives at the North Pole, with a large number of magical elves, and nine (originally eight) flying reindeer. Since the 20th century, in an idea popularized by the 1934 song "Santa Claus Is Coming to Town", Santa Claus has been believed to make a list of children throughout the world, categorizing them according to their behavior ("naughty" or "nice") and to deliver presents, including toys, and candy to all of the well-behaved children in the world, and sometimes coal to the naughty children, on the single night of Christmas Eve. He accomplishes this feat with the aid of the elves who make the toys in the workshop and the reindeer who pull his sleigh.

Christmas (Old English: Crīstesmæsse, meaning "Christ's Mass") is an annual commemoration of the birth of Jesus Christ and a widely observed holiday, celebrated on December 25 by people around the world. A feast central to the Christian liturgical year, it closes the Advent season and initiates the twelve days of Christmastide. Christmas is a civil holiday in many of the world's nations, is celebrated by an increasing number of non-Christians, and is an integral part of the Christmas and holiday season.

The precise date of Jesus' birth, which some historians place between 7 and 2 BC, is unknown.By the early-to-mid 4th century, the Western Christian Church had placed Christmas on December 25, a date later adopted in the East. The date of Christmas may have initially been chosen to correspond with the day exactly nine months after early Christians believed Jesus to have been conceived, as well as the date of the southern solstice (i.e., the Roman winter solstice), with a sun connection being possible because Christians consider Jesus to be the "Sun of righteousness" prophesied in Malachi 4:2. The original date of the celebration in Eastern Christianity was January 6, in connection with Epiphany, and that is still the date of the celebration for the Armenian Apostolic Church and in Armenia, where it is a public holiday. As of 2012, there is a difference of 13 days between the modern Gregorian calendar and the older Julian calendar. Those who continue to use the Julian calendar or its equivalents thus celebrate December 25 and January 6 on what for the majority of the world is January 7 and January 19. For this reason, Ethiopia, Russia, Ukraine,

Serbia, the Republic of Macedonia, and the Republic of Moldova celebrate Christmas on what in the Gregorian calendar is January 7; all the Greek Orthodox Churches celebrate Christmas on December 25. The popular celebratory customs associated in various countries with Christmas have a mix of pre-Christian, Christian and secular themes and origins. Popular modern customs of the holiday include gift giving, Christmas music and caroling, an exchange of Christmas cards, church celebrations, a special meal, and the display of various Christmas decorations, including Christmas trees, Christmas lights, nativity scenes, garlands, wreaths, mistletoe, and holly. In addition, several closely related and often interchangeable figures, known as Santa Claus, Father Christmas, Saint Nicholas and Christkind, are associated with bringing gifts to children during the Christmas season and have their own body of traditions and lore. Because gift-giving and many other aspects of the Christmas festival involve heightened economic activity among both Christians and non-Christians, the holiday has become a significant event and a key sales period for retailers and businesses. The economic impact of Christmas is a factor that has grown steadily over the past few centuries in many regions of the world.

Christmas Day is celebrated as a major festival and public holiday in countries around the world, including many whose populations are mostly non-Christian. In some non-Christian countries, periods of former colonial rule introduced the celebration (e.g. Hong Kong); in others, Christian minorities or foreign cultural influences have led populations to observe the holiday. Countries such as Japan, where Christmas is popular despite there being only a small number of Christians, have adopted many of the secular aspects of Christmas, such as gift-giving, decorations and Christmas trees.

Countries in which Christmas is not a formal public holiday include China, (excepting Hong Kong and Macao), Japan, Saudi Arabia, Algeria, Thailand, Nepal, Iran, Turkey and North Korea. Christmas celebrations around the world can vary markedly in form, reflecting differing cultural and national traditions. Among countries with a strong Christian tradition, a variety of Christmas celebrations have developed that incorporate regional and local cultures. For Christians, participating in a religious service plays an important part in the recognition of the season. Christmas, along with Easter, is the period of highest annual church attendance. In Catholic countries, people hold religious processions or parades in the days preceding Christmas. In other countries, secular processions or parades featuring Santa Claus and other seasonal figures are often held. Family reunions and the exchange of gifts are a widespread feature of the season. Gift giving takes place on Christmas Day in most countries. Others practice gift giving on December 6, Saint Nicholas Day, and January 6, Epiphany.

If a greeting card with Santa Claus is too complicated for your students age group, offer more simple image for A Greeting card with the Christmas tree's décor:

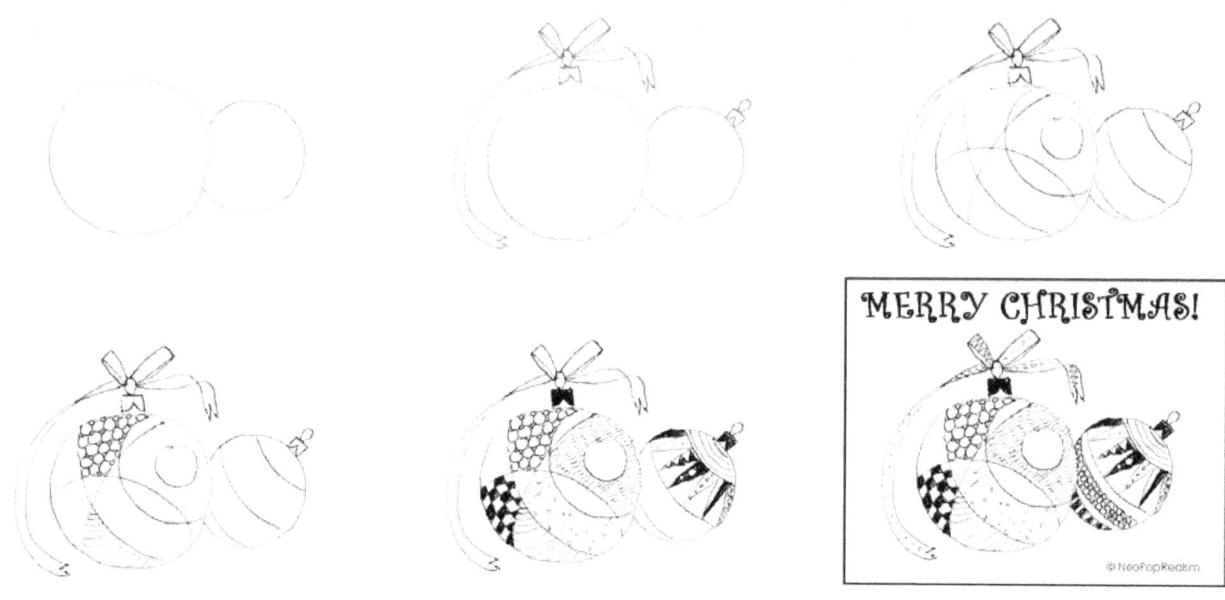

Post card drawing step-by-step

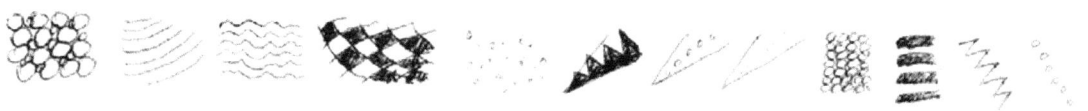

Repetitive patterns used in "Merry Christmas! Greeting card (above)

RESOURCES:

1. Information on NeoPopRealism ink pen/ pattern drawing, its concept and Nadia Russ, who created this style in 1989: see page 101 and http://neopoprealismblackwhiteink.blogspot.com/

2. Wall decals with NeoPopRealism ink pen drawings at 33% off for educators: www.neopoprealism.net

3. A book "*How to Draw Advanced NeoPopRealism Ink Images*", ISBN: 978-0615569758 contains a few teaching projects with step-by-step images and patterns drawing instructions, much more:

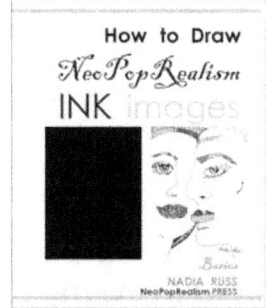

Read this book's review written by the art professional/educator:
http://howtodrawneopoprealism.blogspot.com/2011/10/new-series-of-teaching-books-how-to.html

A book "*NeoWhimsies: NeoPopRealism Ink Drawing Basics for Mannequins*", ISBN: 978-0615651859 contains 10 teaching projects/ lesson plans with step-by-step drawing instructions, more:

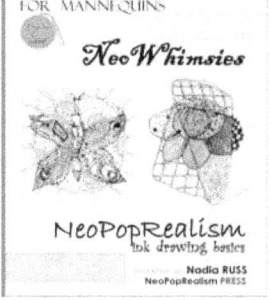

Short review: http://howtodrawneopoprealism.blogspot.com/2012/07/both-books-how-to-draw-advanced.html

4. Photographs or prints with the realistic drawings of Santa Claus or Christmas tree decoration (fin online).

FOLLOW UP ACTVITIES:
View Nadia Russ' NeoPopRealism artwork online and discuss NeoPopRealism ink pen pattern drawing style.
Name artists who were the best representatives and inventors of new styles of visual arts:
Monet - Impressionism,
Dali - Surrealism,
Picasso - Cubism,
Andy Warhol and Jasper Johns - Pop Art,
Jeff Koons - Neo-Pop,
Nadia Russ - NeoPopRealism.

Fight bullying in schools to live with dignity with help of NeoPopRealism philosophy and 10 canons for happier life (see page 101).

Art lesson plan 14

Creating Mardi Gras NeoPopRealist Mask with Ink Pen /Pattern Drawing inspired by Nadia Russ

GRADES: 6-8, 9-12, adapt. 3-5
SUBJECT: Visual Arts, Crafts & Music.

This art lesson focuses on the NeoPopRealism abstract and the repetitive patterns drawing used to create the Mardi Gras NeoPopRealist Mask for carnivals

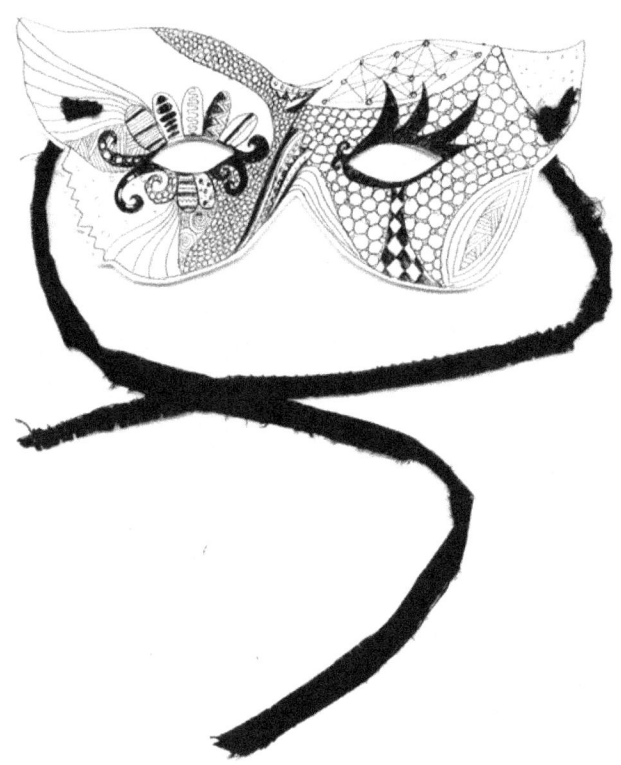

OBJECTIVES:
Students will
- learn (or be reminded) about NeoPopRealism ink pen / pattern drawing style/ concept and work of artist Nadia Russ, who created this style in 1989 (see Resources).
- define the term "NeoPopRealism" and differentiate NeoPopRealism ink pen pattern drawing

and the realism drawing approach.

- experiment with drawing of the NeoPopRealism abstract - the repetitive patterns.
- create/draw a Mardi Gras NeoPopRealist Mask for carnival, inspired by Nadia Russ and NeoPopRealism, using ink pen black.

Material:
- 1 piece 5.5"x8.5" of white thick cardboard for creating a Mardi Gras NeoPopRealist Mask
- white paper 8.5" x 11" for experimenting with the repetitive patterns drawing
- 2 thin ribbons, each 12 inch long
- ink pen black 0.7 mm thin
- scissors
- computer

Day 1:
Display in classroom posters with Nadia Russ' NeoPopRealism ink pen pattern drawings (see RESOURCES) or show her NeoPopRealist drawings online.
Introduce (or remind) the NeoPopRealism ink pen pattern drawing concept and how Nadia Russ created it in 1989, see page 101 and http://neopoprealismblackwhiteink.blogspot.com/.
Ask students to compare NeoPopRealism ink pattern drawings by Nadia Russ and drawings by realists-artists such as Rembrandt and Leonardo da Vinci.
Discuss with students Mardi Gras mask, its history, how it decorates and beautifies the carnivals and costumes.

ABOUT MARDI GRAS.
"Mardi Gras", "Mardi Gras season", and "Carnival season", refer to events of the Carnival celebrations, beginning on or after Epiphany and culminating on the day before Ash Wednesday. Mardi Gras arrived in North America as a French Catholic tradition with the Le Moyne brothers, Pierre Le Moyne d'Iberville and Jean-Baptiste Le Moyne de Bienville, in the late 17th century, when King Louis XIV sent the pair to defend France's claim on the territory of Louisiane, which included what are now the U.S. states of Alabama, Mississippi, and Louisiana. The expedition, led by Iberville, entered the mouth of the Mississippi River on the evening of March 2, 1699, Lundi Gras. They did not yet know it was the river explored and claimed for France by René-Robert Cavelier, Sieur de La Salle in 1683. The party proceeded upstream to a place on the west bank about 60 miles downriver from where New Orleans is today, and made camp. This was on March 3, 1699, Mardi Gras, so in honor of this holiday, Iberville named the spot Point du Mardi Gras (French: "Mardi Gras Point") and called the nearby tributary Bayou Mardi Gras. Bienville went on to found the settlement of Mobile, Alabama in 1702 as the first capital of French Louisiana. In 1703 French settlers in Mobile established the first organized Mardi Gras celebration tradition in what was to become the United States. While Mardi Gras in the United States is not observed nationally across the country, a number of cities and regions in the U.S. have notable Carnival celebrations. The earliest Carnival celebrations occurred in Mobile, Biloxi, New Orleans, and Pensacola, which have each developed separate traditions. In addition, modern activities generally vary from city to city across the U.S.. Costumes and masks are frequently worn on Mardi Gras

Day. Laws against concealing one's identity with a mask are suspended for the day. Banks are closed, and some businesses and other places with security concerns (such as convenience stores) post signs asking people to remove their masks before entering. Mardi Gras is composed of various events such as balls for social clubs in the New Orleans Area, but the main event is simply a street festival, open to the public. Some individual krewes do, however, produce an official poster of their organization each year.

Discuss with students the particular mask that they are going to create using a thick white cardboard size 5.5"x8.5". Measure the distance between the eyes and draw the eye's contours that you will cut out later. Then, draw the contour of a mask. Demonstrate the creating of Mardi Gras NeoPopRealist mask step-by-step. Divide a shape of a mask into section;. then fill some sections with different repetitive patterns (see illustration below).

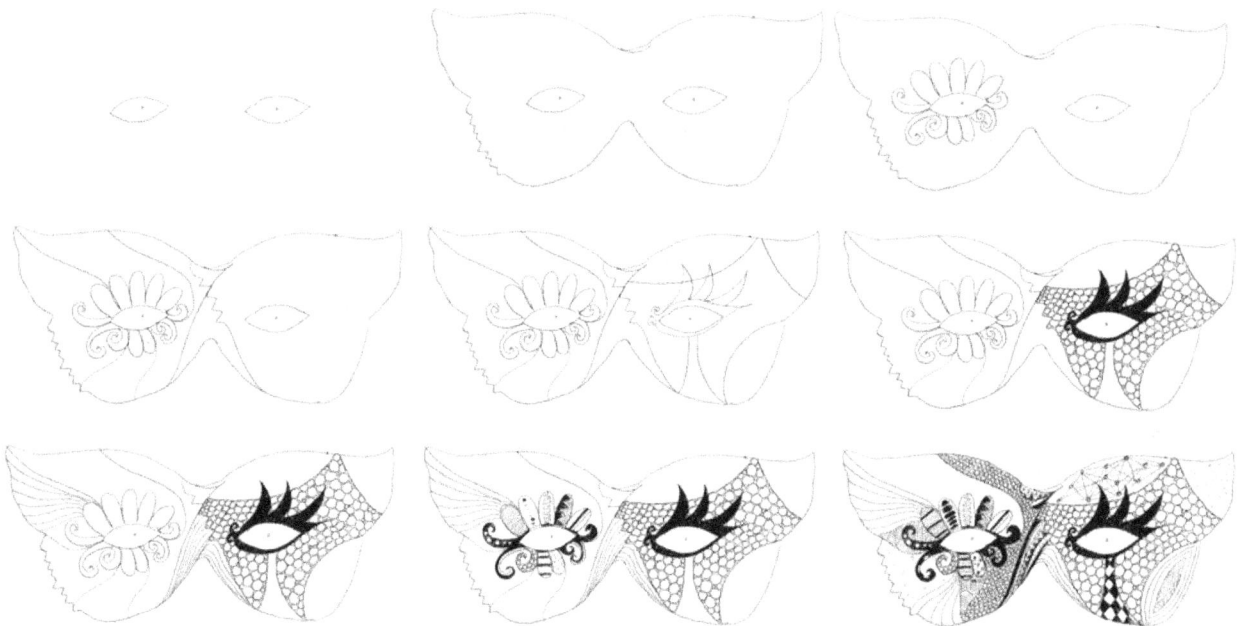

When your drawing process is finished, cut out the mask, make holes at the eyes' areas and small holes for ribbons at the both sides left and right (see image below):

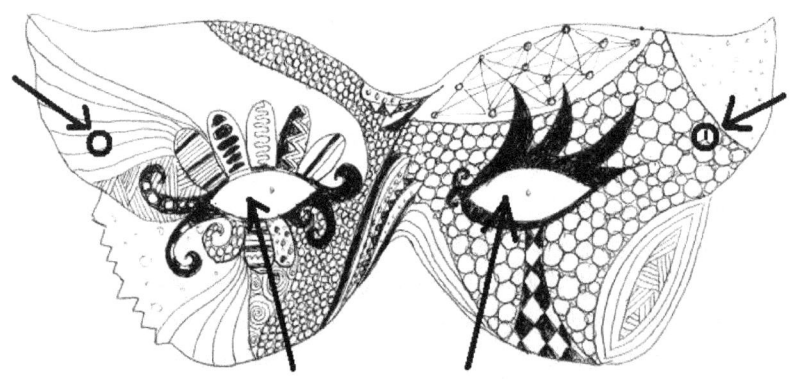

Then, insert into the two small holes on the left and on the right the ribbons, make the knots. Wear the mask.

Offer each student a sheet of white drawing paper 8.5" x 11", divided into squares/section. Turn on the music with syncopation (not loud and preferably jazz). Offer students create in each square/section different repetitive pattern that they would use in their Mardi Gras NeoPopRealist mask. When students draw, they enter meditative state of mind. While creating the patterns, students focus on each element of the pattern creation, they draw slowly, not in a hurry. Ink pen should be thin - 0.7mm, not a thick marker.

Day 2: Remind students the NeoPopRealism ink pen/ pattern drawing concept: A line creates sections, then, these sections filled with different repetitive patterns, some sections can be left blank. Eraser never used. Discuss with students the contrast and flatness of the NeoPopRealism abstract ink pen pattern drawings. Explain why NeoPopRealism drawing needs no eraser: if a 'mistake' made, it visually disappears because the following patterns make this 'mistake' invisible and the whole composition balanced.

Each student create step-by-step one NeoPopRealist Mardi Gras mask on thick white cardboard. First, they measure distance between their eyes and draw eye's contours. Then, they draw a contour of the mask's shape, then divide the mask's shapes into sections as shown in illustrations above. Then, students fill the sections with different repetitive patterns: circles, whirles, lines, squares, zigzags..., some sections they leave blank.

When the drawing process is finished, students cut out the holes in the eyes' areas and the small holes for the ribbons. Then, when the masks are ready they can wear them.

Students compare and discuss their masks, discuss the concept of NeoPopRealism ink pen/ pattern drawing, the patterns they used in their drawings. Students define term "NeoPopRealism". They discuss the Marti Gras carnival.

Teacher demonstrate the best masks in front of the class.

LESSON PLAN - BACKGROUND AND HISTORICAL INFORMATION:
Nadia RUSS is a Ukrainian-born Russian painter/ graphic artist living in the USA, who created a style of visual arts NeoPopRealism. She is famous for innovative NeoPopRealism art and ink pen pattern drawing, including abstract, the meditative style that she created in 1989. Instead of careful copying reality - wild life or human figure, Nadia RUSS creates her artwork using imagination. As Nadia RUSS experimented and developed her distinctive techniques, her drawings became more symbolic. For her drawings she uses white paper and black ink pen. However, sometimes, she uses blue ink on white paper and gold/silver ink on black paper.
How did Nadia RUSS develop her unique and original style NeoPopRealism? RUSS had studied classical drawing and composition since she was a child, but as she studied she found herself drawn to produce less realistic, more imaginative artwork. In 1989, she created NeoPopRealism art

style and ink pattern drawing concept: line creates sections; then, these section filled with different repetitive patterns, some section should be left blank. If artwork made on canvas using color paints and a brush, then, it would be a combination of sections filled with hot and cold color paint, partly with patterns. In 1990, RUSS exhibited her first ink/ pattern drawings in a group exhibition in Moscow's famous Manege. Later, she was exhibiting her artwork in art galleries. In 1996, she moved to the Freeport, Bahamas, where her artwork gained special brightness. In 2000, she came to the USA where she lives till present. Nadia Russ create a term "NeoPopRealism" January 4, 2003. Same year, she manifested her new style of visual arts NeoPopRealism internationally. In 2004, she created NeoPopRealism 10 canons for happier life. In 2006-2007, several US and European museums collected Nadia Russ' paintings and drawings and now, these artworks are in the permanent collections of these museums.

FOLLOW UP ACTIVITIES:
View Nadia Russ artwork online and discuss NeoPopRealism ink pen pattern drawing style. Name artists who invented new styles of visual arts and were best their representatives: Monet - Impressionism, Dali - Surrealism, Picasso - Cubism, Andy Warhol and Jasper Johns - Pop Art, Jeff Koons - Neo-Pop, Nadia Russ - NeoPopRealism.

All illustrations here are given not to copy them, but to examine them and then create with students their own, unique pieces. The copying kills your and your students imagination and creative abilities. However, our purpose is to increase and develop your and your students imagination and the artistic abilities.

RECOMMENDED BOOKS:
A book with 10 step-by-step projects / lesson plans: *"NeoWhimsies: NeoPopRealism ink Drawing Basics for Mannequins"*, ISBN: 9780615651859.

RESOURCES:

- Wall decals with NeoPopRealism ink pen drawings at 33% off for educators:
www.neopoprealism.net

- Information on NeoPopRealism ink pen/ pattern drawing, its concept and Nadia Russ' biography, who created this style in 1989: see page 101 and http://neopoprealismblackwhiteink.blogspot.com/

Fight bullying in school with NeoPopRealism philosophy for happy life, see 10 canons in www.nadiaruss.com or page 101.

Art Lesson Plan 15

Imaginative/Abstract NeoPopRealism ink pen / pattern drawing: Chess Board

GRADES: can be adapted for 3-5, 6-8, 9-12
DURATION: lesson may be carried over to another day(s)

This imagination/ abstract lesson plan employs four concepts: contextual information and research, questioning, reflection, and artwork-making.

GOAL:
This lesson plan is designed to develop imaginative thinking and creative actions, to lead students to innovative results and prepare for greater in-depth learning in different subject areas.
After viewing, analyzing and executing the imaginative work of art, the goal is to lead students to a synthesis that helps acquire a deeper understanding.
Support imaginative learning in classroom, participate in the learning.

OBJECTIVES:
Students will
- use imagination to create the NeoPopReaism ink pen/pattern drawings/ squares on paper 8"x11"
- exercise/prepare yourself to draw the squares/designs on the thick cardboard, creating a chess board
- develop measuring/estimation skills
- represent self through symbols and images
- create from the thick piece of cardboard the custom chess board with NeoPopRealism ink pen pattern drawings/ squares (instead of just dark squares)
- spray the surface of the board with the clear varnish, when completing the work.

MATERIALS:
- the thick piece of white cardboard (square shape) for creating a chess board (can be different size)
- white drawing paper 8.5"x11"
- black thin ink pen 0.7 mm (not marker)
- clear vanish spray for paper

THE PROCEDURE:

Day 1.
Explain (or remind if students already familiar) the concept of the NeoPopRealism ink pen/ pattern

drawing.

Draw the lines inside of each square that create sections. Then, fill these sections with different repetitive patterns (see illustrations below).

Demonstrate how different types of line's turns and repetitive patterns can change images characters. When you/ students draw the line and patterns, you use imagination, it is unconscious process. This drawing process is meditative. You teach students not to copy but to create new imaginative compositions and new imaginative patterns' combinations.

Offered below drawings are not to copy them, but to examine and to learn the creative process step-by-step. Copying kills imagination. Never copy others' drawings. However, students can draw texture, looking at the nature or the objects they see around, in the real life. Regularly, when you draw your ink pen/ patterns drawings-abstracts, avoid using the square shape paper because the square is limiting you, adding the heavy restrictions as if you were putting your creativity into a "prison" of a space. The square is limiting your imagination and potentials to create the versatile images, expressing yourself the best ways you can. Choose the rectangular size of paper, it gives you an opportunity to be unlimited and unique in forms, using your fantasy and imagination without any restrictions from outside.

This particular project uses the squares only as the fragments of a bigger arts/crafts project.

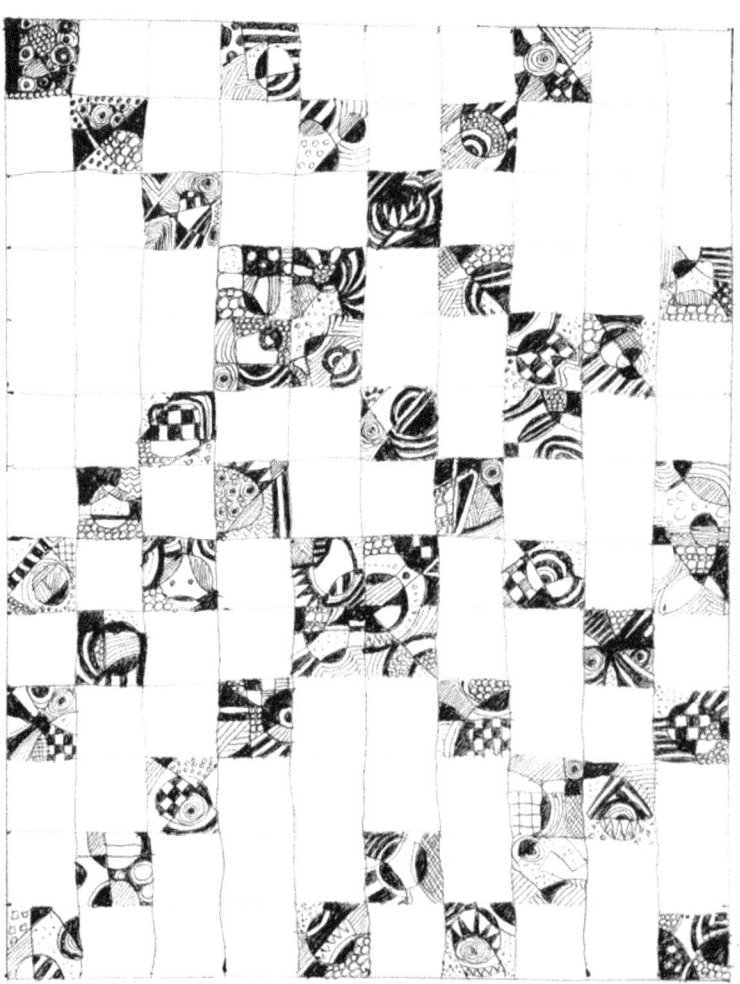

Teach students to create many different and unique abstract images using imagination, to combine them together into one image/ project.

Explain that often the use of same and simple repetitive patterns results in the absolutely different and unique images.

See enlarged square images visual instructions at http://neopoprealismartlessonplans.blogspot.com/.

Have students divide the 8.5"x11" piece of paper into small squares/sections as shown on the illustrations below.

Have students fill some squares/ sections with unique designs. Make sure students fill each square with different design, using their imagination, without copying previous or other people's designs.

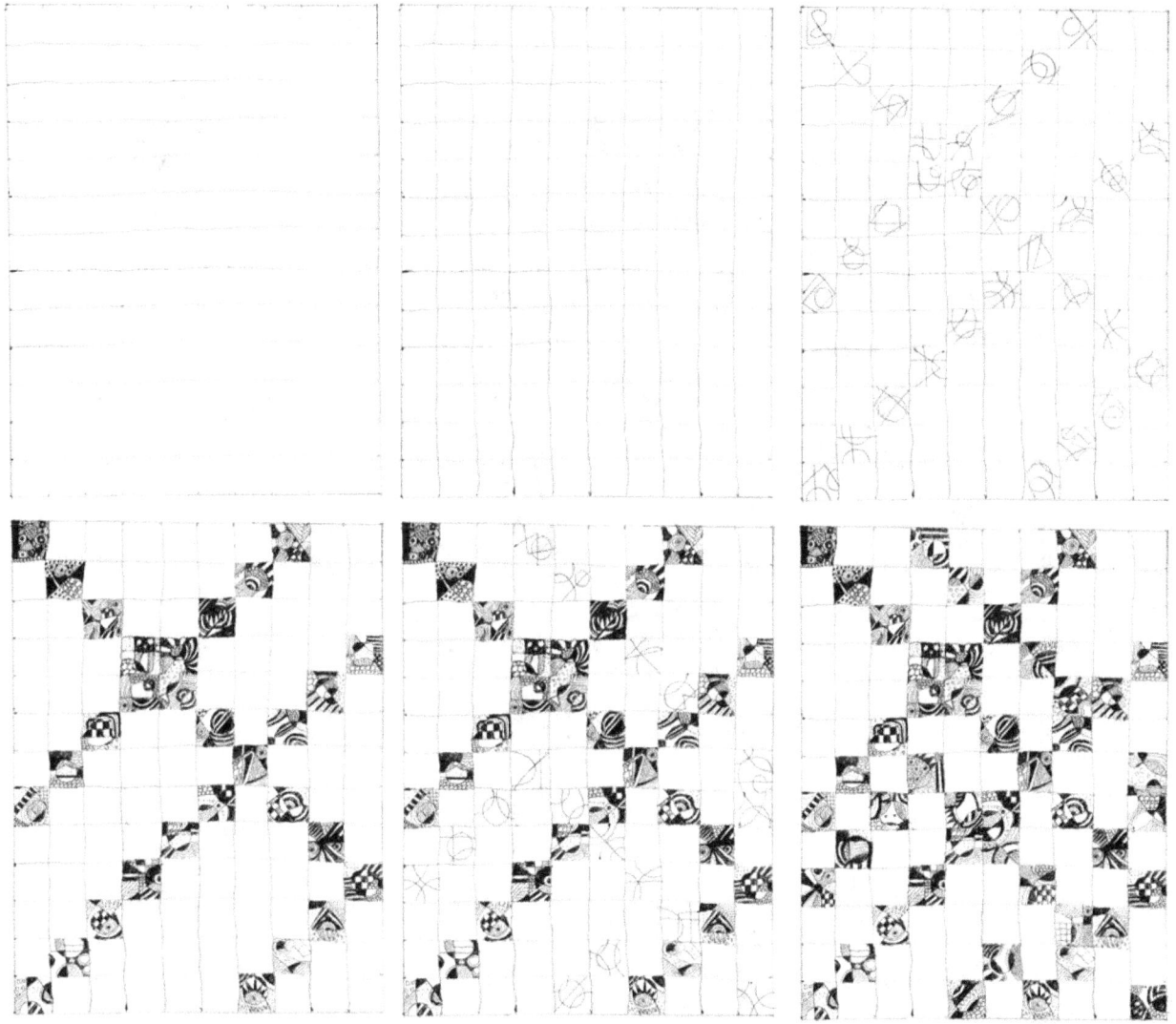

ABOUT ABSTRACT N VISUAL ARTS.

Abstract in visual arts refers to an object or image which has been distilled from the real world.

Artwork that reshapes the natural world for expressive purposes is called abstract; that which derives from, but does not imitate a recognizable subject is called nonobjective abstraction. In the 20th century the trend toward abstraction coincided with advances in science, technology, and changes in urban life, eventually reflecting an interest in psychoanalytic theory. Later still, abstraction was manifest in more purely formal terms, such as freedom from objective context, and a reduction of form to basic geometric designs.

In 1989, Nadia Russ created new style of visual arts and the NeoPopRealist abstract way of ink pen pattern drawing. This NeoPopRealism abstract ink pen/ pattern drawing style is created through the combination of seemed chaotically appeared different patterns' sections. However, this "chaos" turns into the harmonic abstract compositions.

Day 2
Explain students what is the Chess game and its brief history (see page 79).

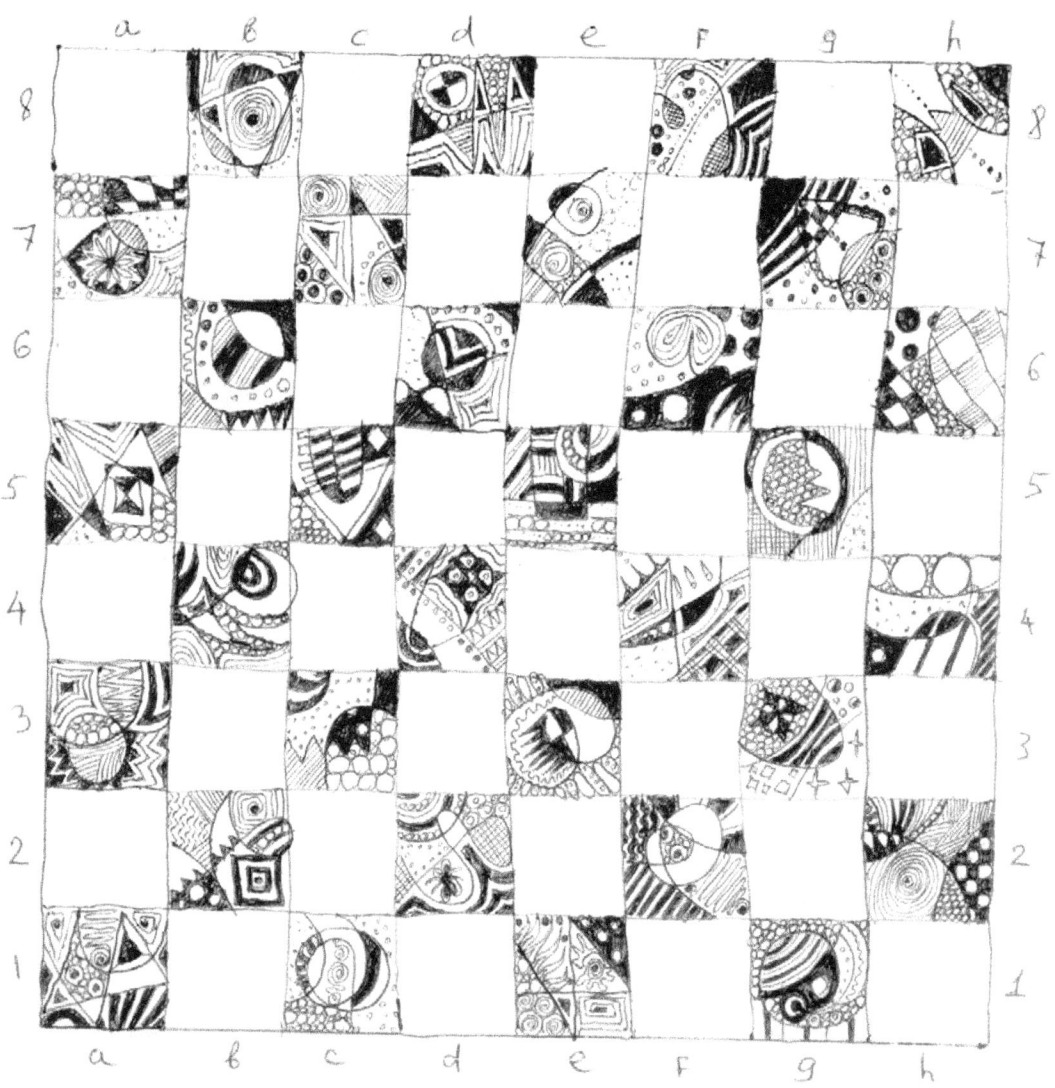

Have students measure and divide the thick cardboard into 64 same size squares, as if it would be the chess board.

Have student create in 32 squares the different designs (see/ examine illustrations above), read more at http://neopoprealismartlessonplans.blogspot.com/2012/11/neopoprealism-abstract-neowhimsies-gr-6.html/.

Have students spray the surface with a clear vanish for paper. Chess' figures students can use from the old chess they have at home.

Compare the students' chess boards, display the best work. Discuss the results from artistic point of view.

Give information about where students can learn the chess game (find information about local chess clubs online).

ABOUT NEOPOPREALISM INK PEN PATTERN DRAWING STYLE:

Nadia Russ created NeoPopRealism in 1989. She loves to draw faces, and this kind of abstract ink pen/ patterns drawing (combinations of different patterns in sections) she always included in her ink artworks as the background since 1989 up until now. This drawing is meditative. When you draw the repetitive patterns, you enter the meditative state of mind, the highest state in which our mind can exist. It increases your learning and creative abilities.

January 4, 2003 Nadia Russ created a term to name her new and unique style - NeoPopRealism. In 2004, a few swindlers and craftsmen, who did not know that all Nadia Russ' achievements since early 90s were documented, decided to present themselves as the "creators" of this ink pen/ pattern drawing style. This infamous and at the same time comedic story began in 2002, when Nadia Russ lived in Florida, renting from one of the shameless and hungry for $ swindlers an apartment on the beach...The whole story about it and more about her dynamic life she tells in a book, in autobiographical nonfiction "DECA-DaNCE", ISBN: 978-0615655680, published in 2012 and available at Amazon and through other stores.

Read more about NeoPopRealism ink pen/ pattern drawing and its concept at the end of this book, page 101.

ABOUT CHESS GAME

Chess known as "the game of kings." It can raise your IQ. Because the brain works like a muscle, it needs exercise like any bicep or quad to be healthy - chess exercises both sides of the brain. Chess game greatly increases originality and creativity. It improves memory, increases problem-solving skills, improves reading skills, concentration. It grows dendrites. It develops parts of the brain, responsible for planning, judgment, and self-control.

Chess is a two-player strategy board game played on a chessboard, a square checkered gameboard with 64 squares arranged in an eight-by-eight grid. It is one of the world's most popular games, played by millions of people at home, clubs, online, by correspondence, and in tournaments. Each player begins the game with sixteen pieces: one king, one queen, two rooks, two knights, two bishops, and eight pawns. Each of the six piece types moves differently. Pieces are used to attack and capture the opponent's pieces, with the objective to 'checkmate' the opponent's king by placing it under an inescapable threat of capture. In addition to checkmate, the game can be won by the voluntary resignation of the opponent, which typically occurs when too much material is lost, or if checkmate appears unavoidable. A game may also result in a draw in several ways, where neither player wins. The course of the game is divided into three phases: opening, middlegame, and endgame.

The history of chess spans some 1500 years. The earliest predecessors of the game originated in India, before the 6th century AD. From India, the game spread to Persia. When the Arabs conquered Persia, chess was taken up by the Muslim world and subsequently spread to Southern Europe. In Europe, chess evolved into roughly its current form in the 15th century. In the second half of the 19th century, modern chess tournament play began, and the first world Chess Championship was held in 1886. The 20th century saw great leaps forward in chess theory and the establishment of the World Chess Federation (FIDE). Developments in the 21st century include use of computers for analysis, which originated in the 1970s with the first programmed chess games on the market. Online gaming appeared in the mid-1990s.

FOLLOW UP ACTIVITIES:
View Nadia Russ artwork online and in books, discuss NeoPopRealism ink pen / pattern drawing style. Name some artists who were best representatives and invented new styles of visual arts:
Monet - Impressionism,
Dali - Surrealism,
Picasso - Cubism,
Andy Warhol and Jasper Johns - Pop Art,
Jeff Koons - Neo-Pop,
Nadia Russ - NeoPopRealism.

RESOURCES:

- Wall decals with NeoPopRealism ink pen drawings at 33% off for educators: www.neopoprealism.net

- Information on NeoPopRealism ink pen/ pattern drawing, its concept and Nadia Russ' biography, who created this style in 1989: see page 101 and http://neopoprealismblackwhiteink.blogspot.com/

Fight bullying in school with NeoPopRealism philosophy, see 10 canons for happier life in page 101 or www.nadiaruss.com.

Templates for Training & Experimenting

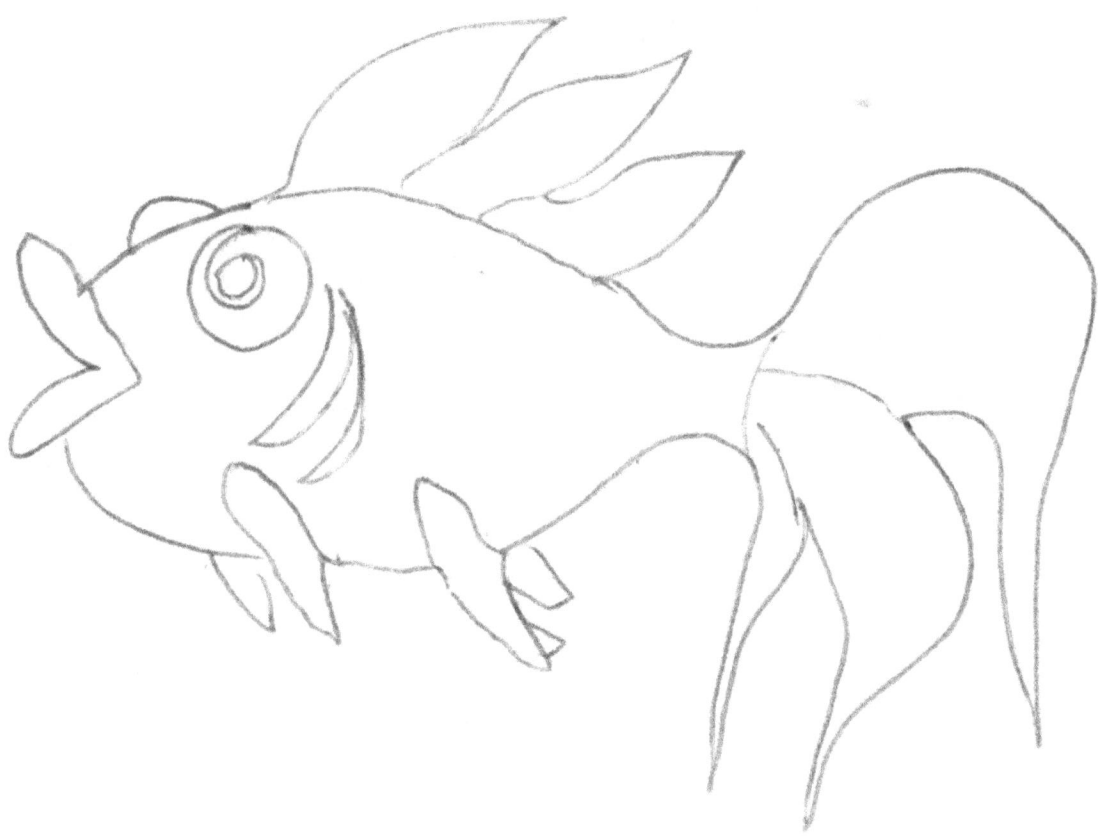

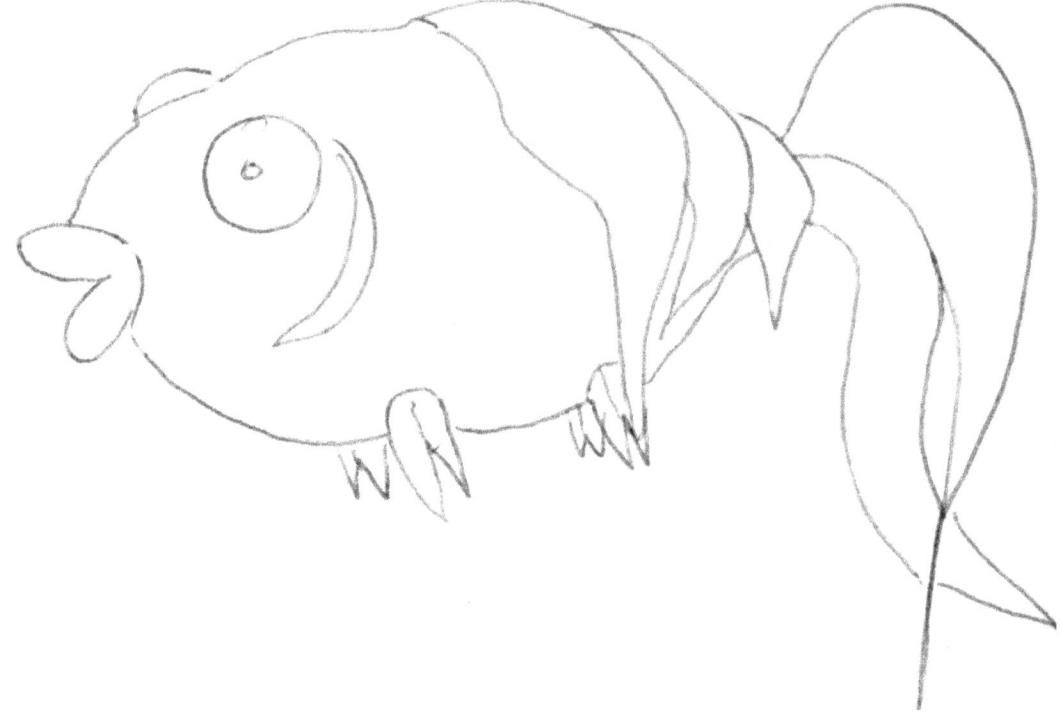

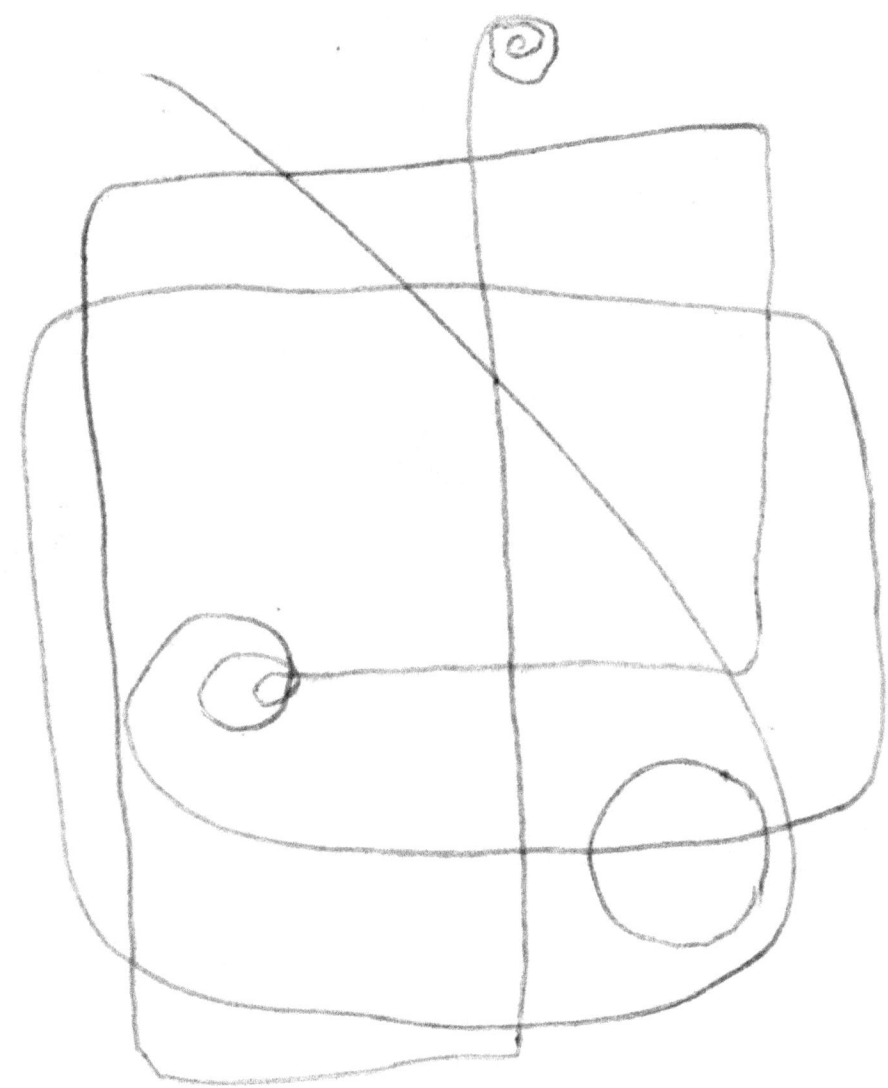

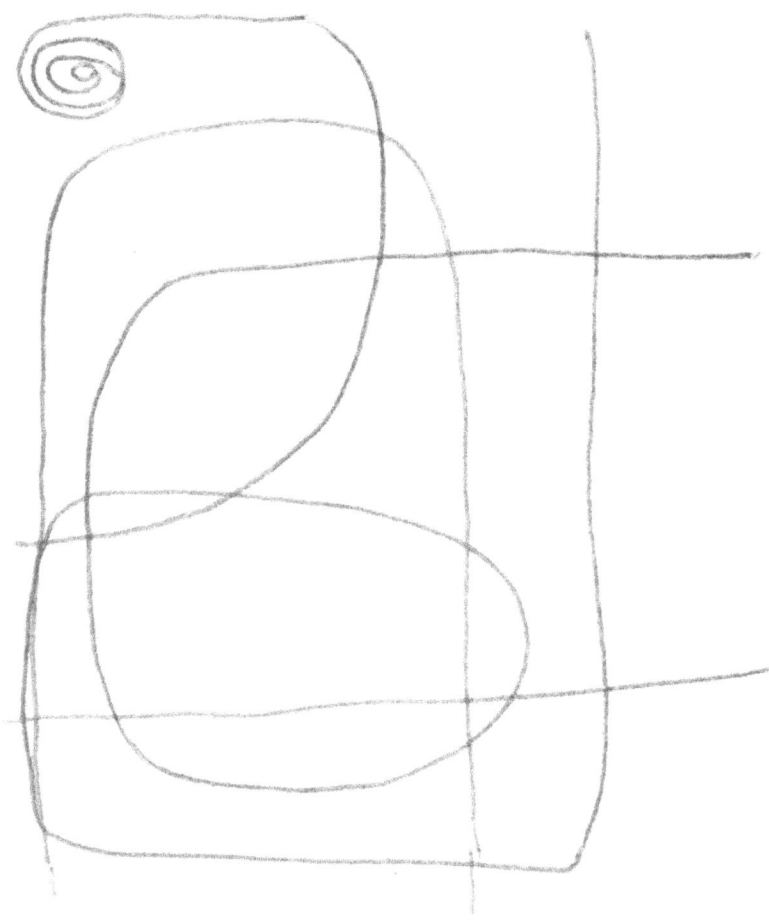

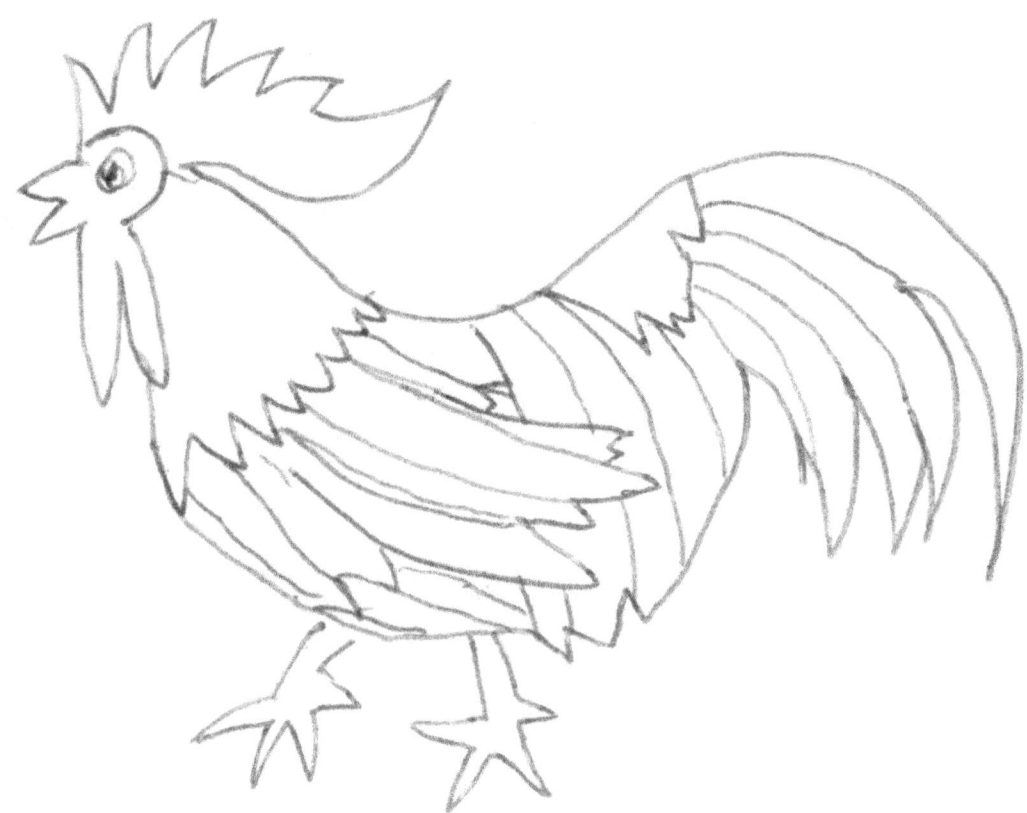

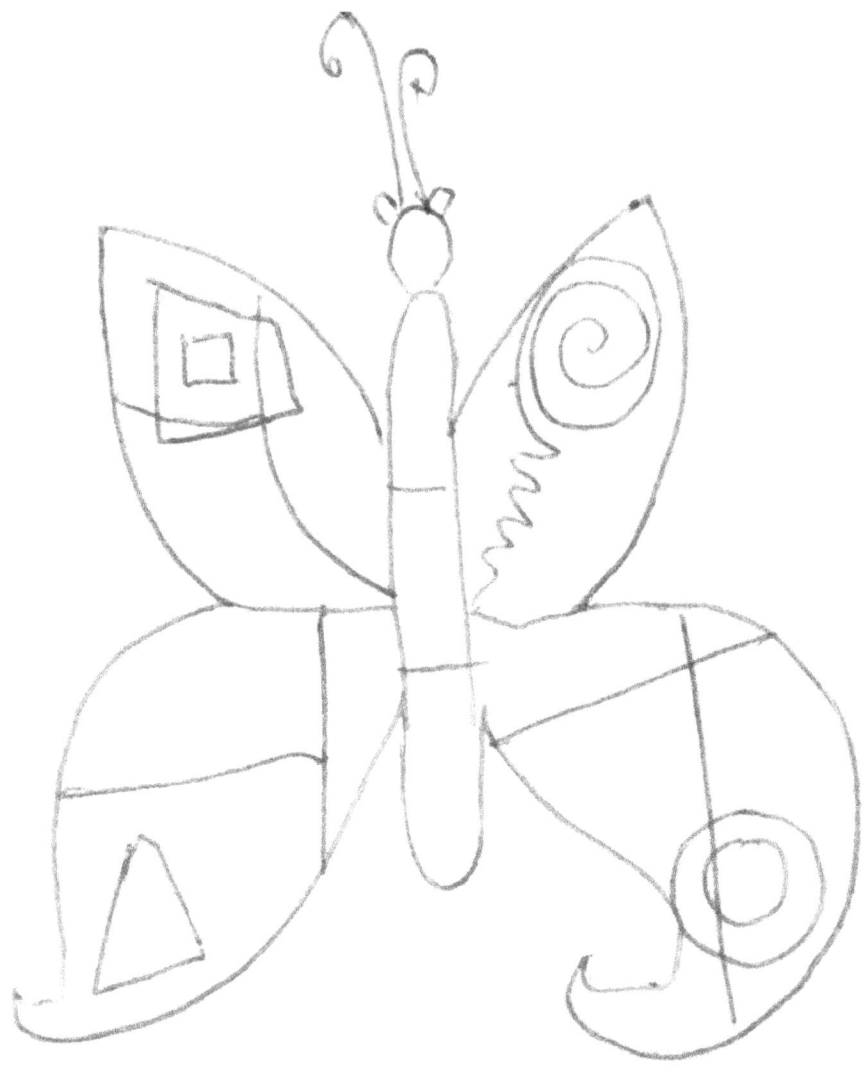

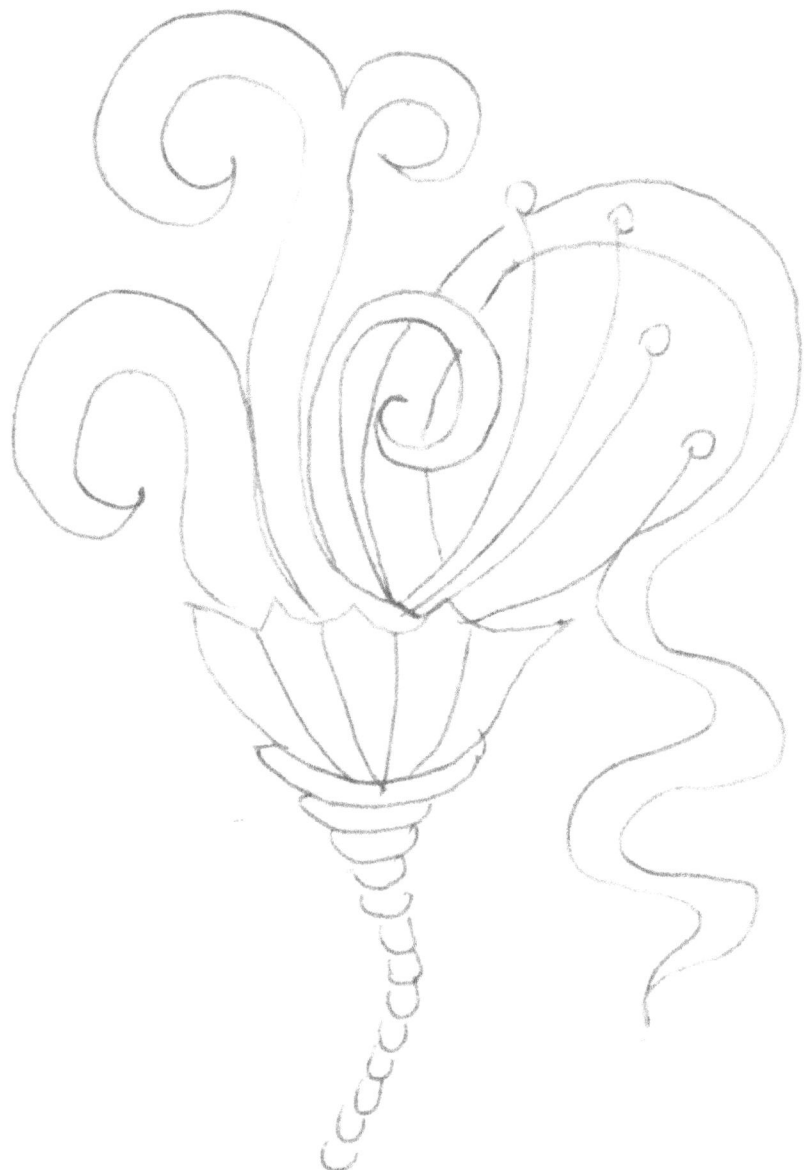

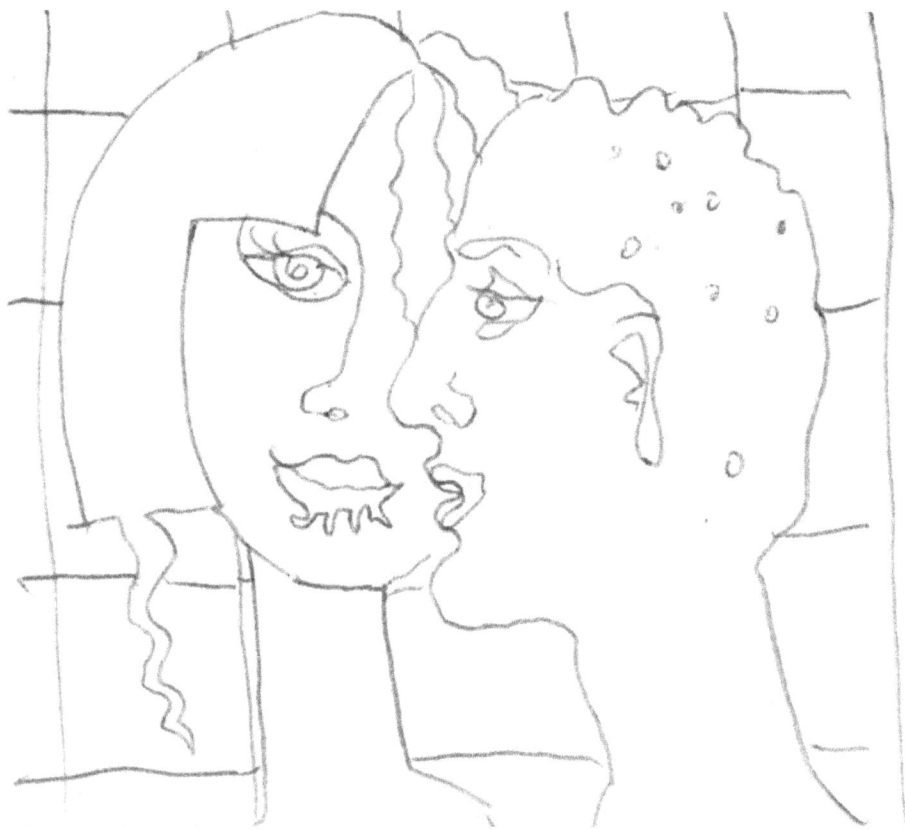

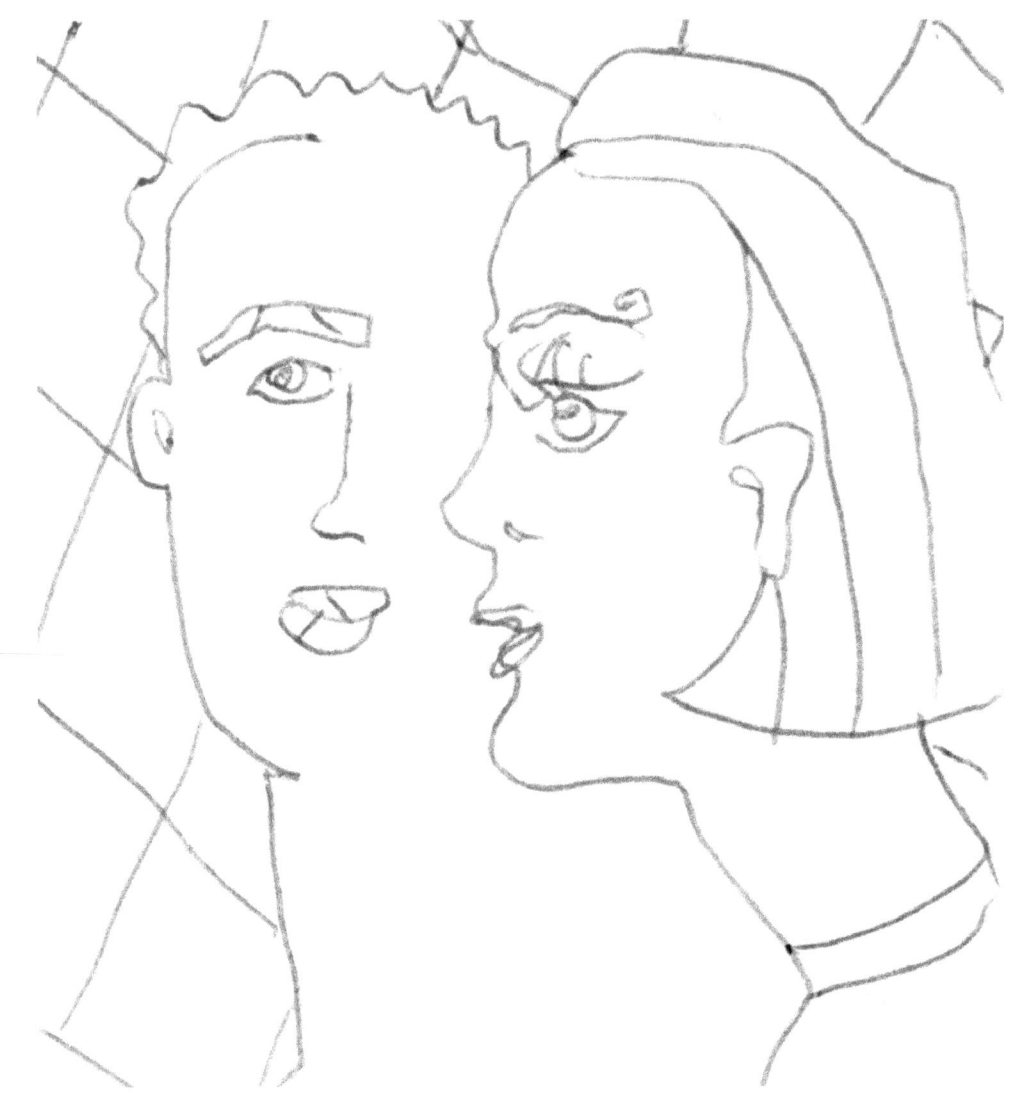

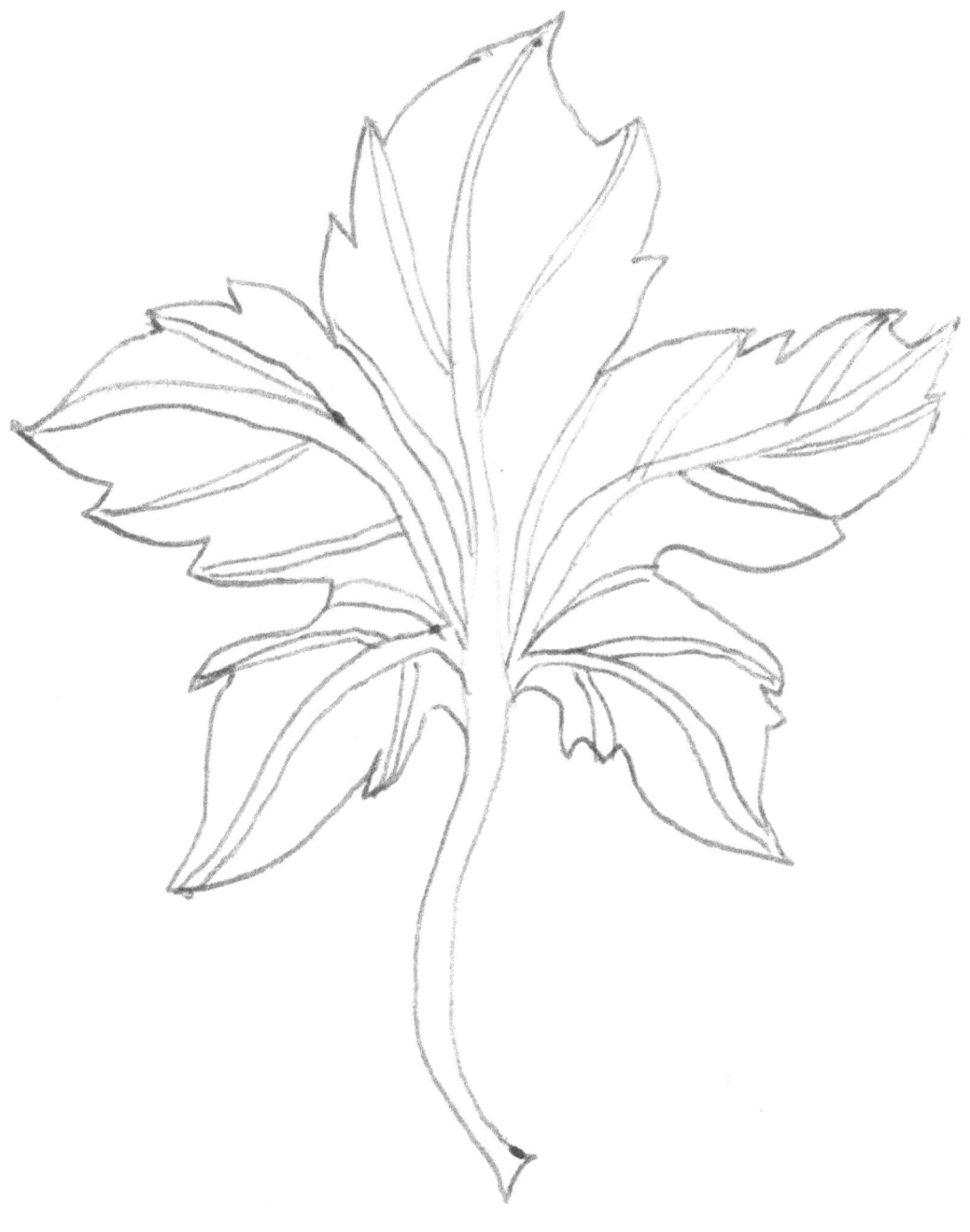

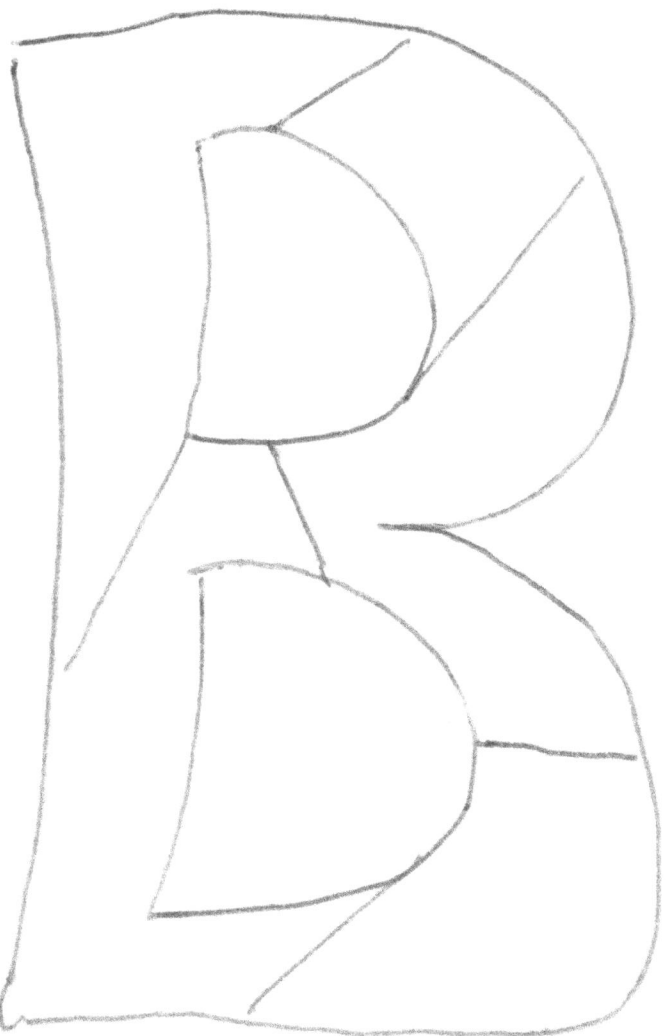

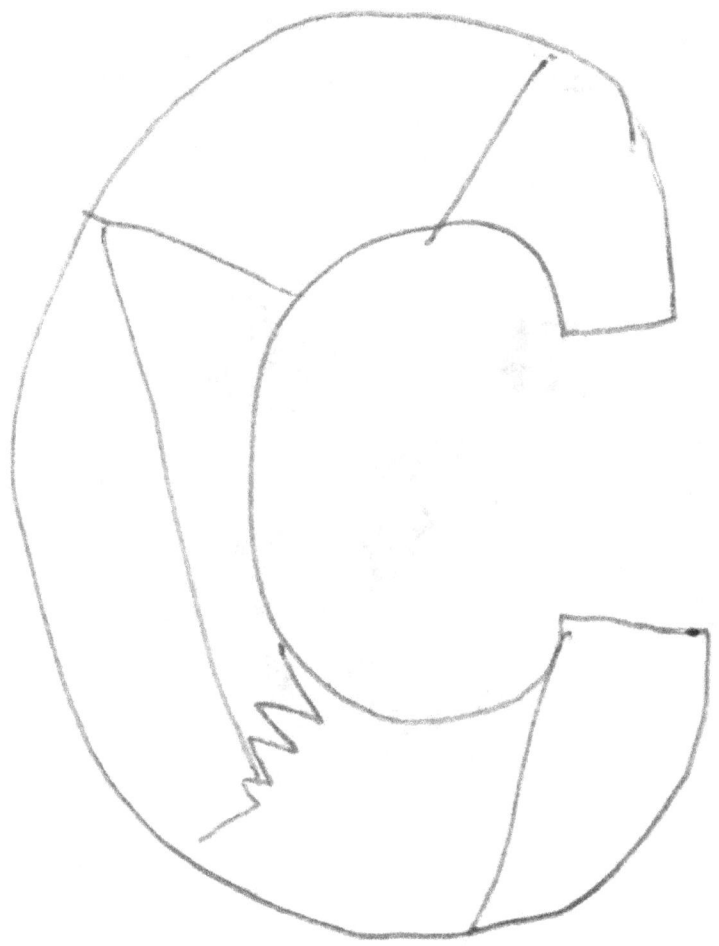

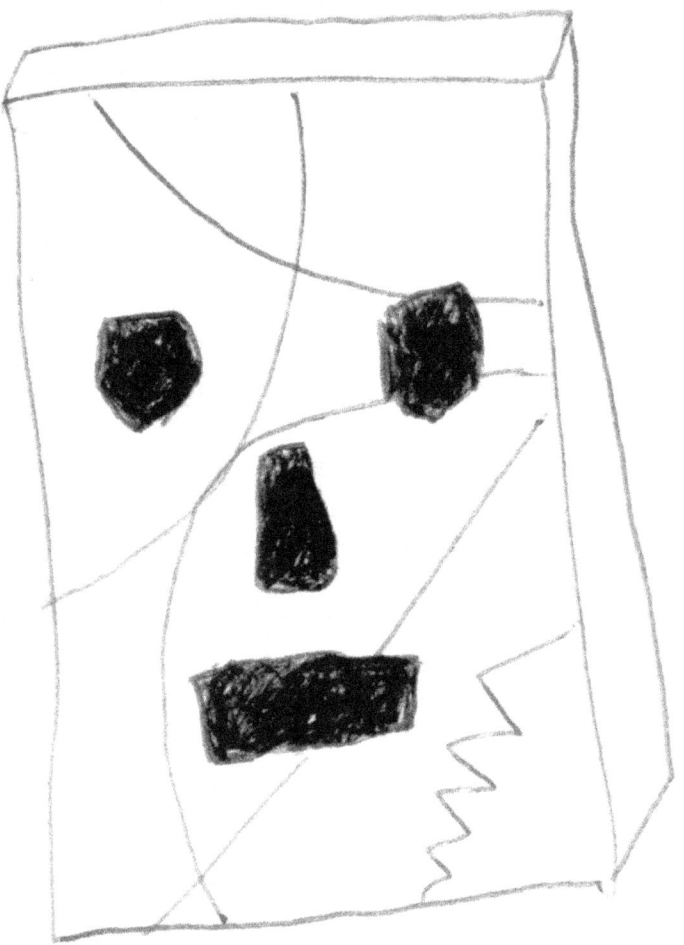

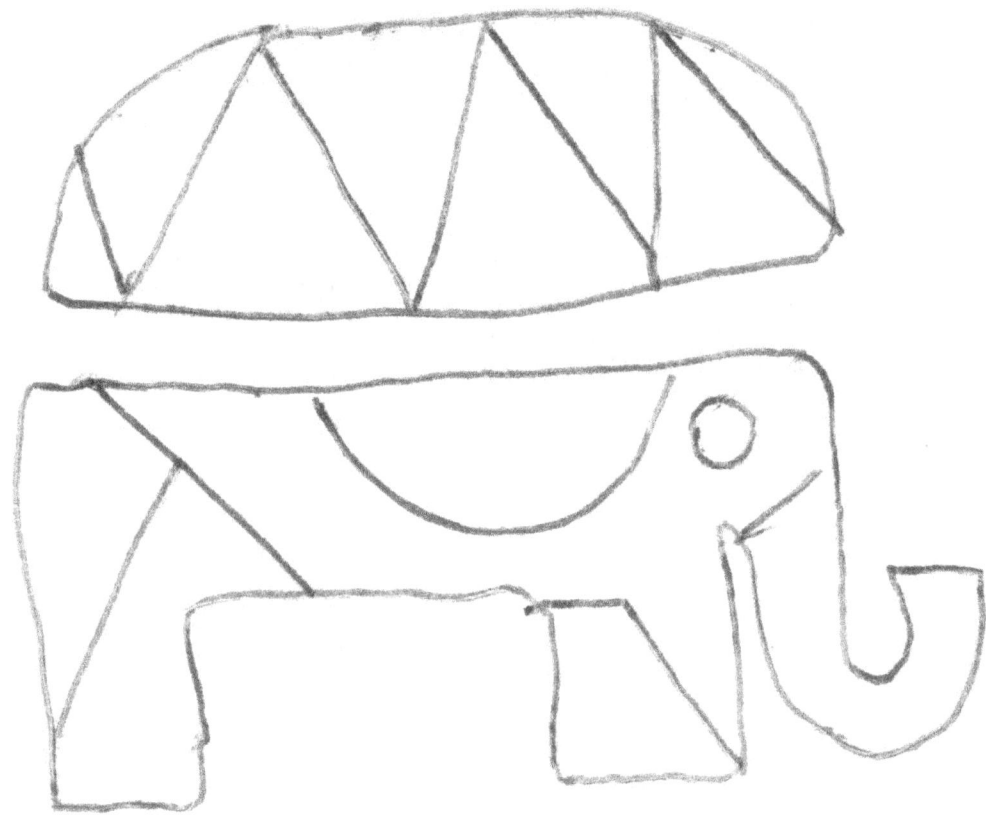

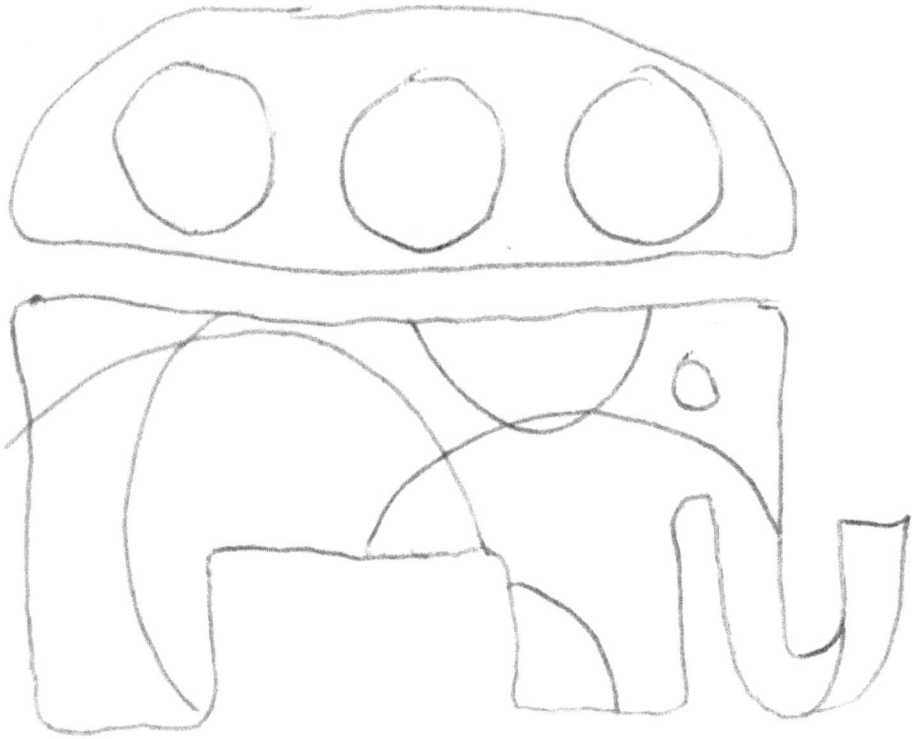

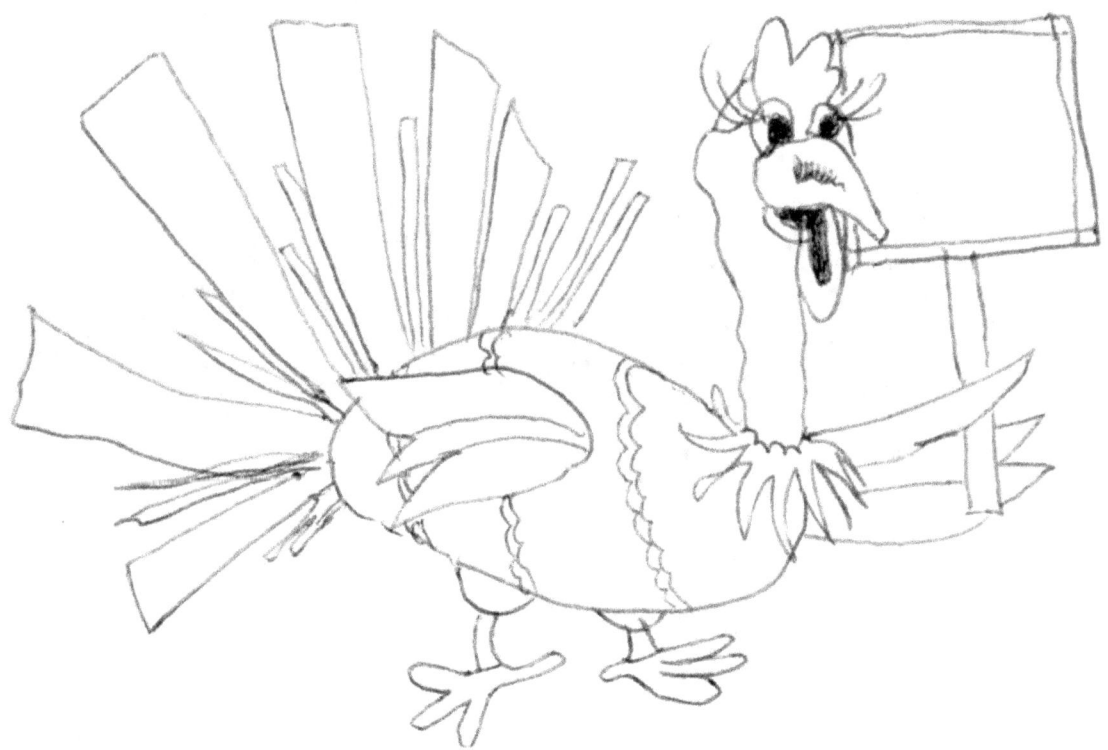

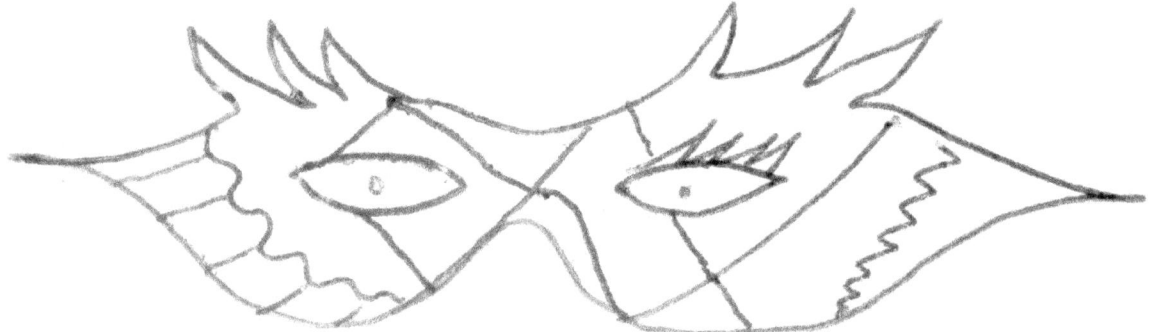

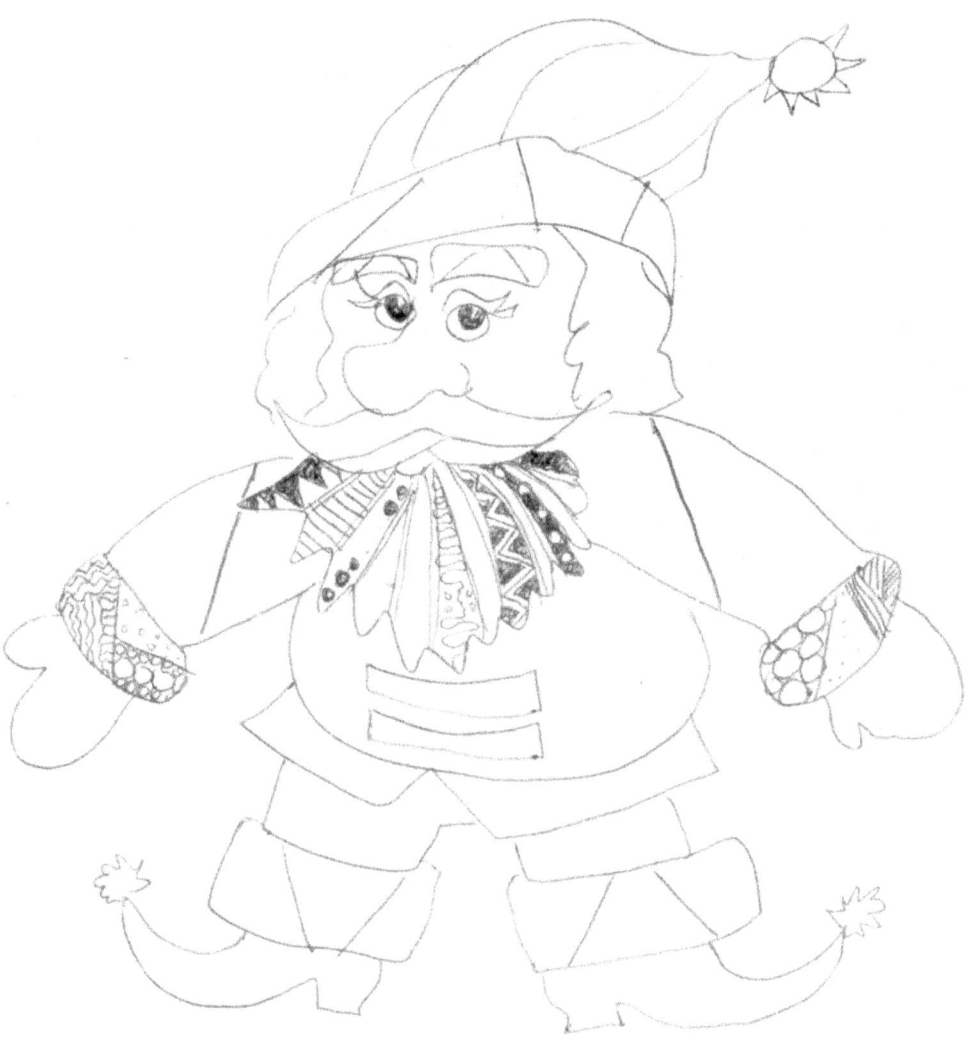

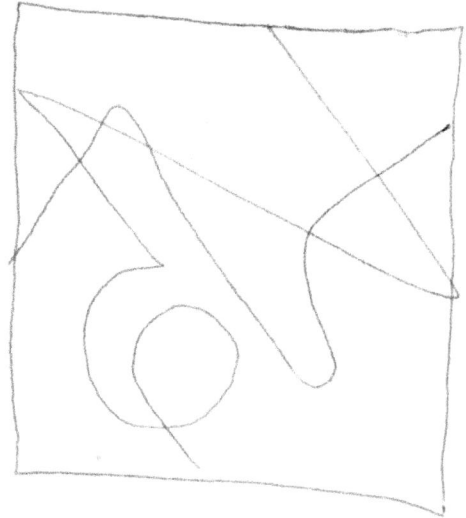

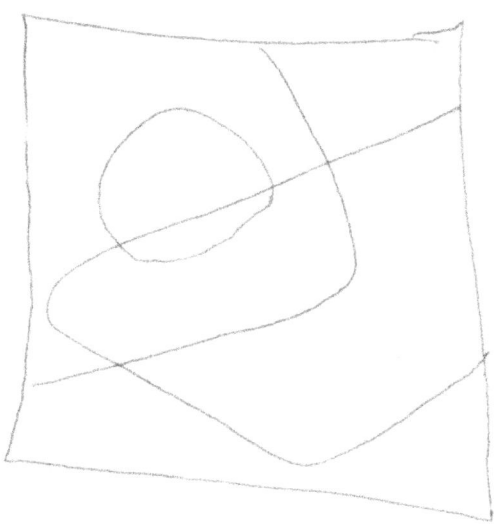

Nadia Russ' NeoPopRealism Ink Pen Pattern Drawings History

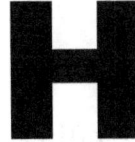er ink pen pattern drawing concept Nadia Russ created in 1989. Nadia Russ loves jazz.

One day, she entered the meditative state of mind and began to draw ink pen / pattern images. They were different than the ordinary realistic images. A line created sections, section Nadia filled with different repetitive patterns. How this would be connected to jazz, you may ask. Jazz and Nadia Russ' NeoPopRealism ink pen /pattern drawings are based on syncopation and accents that appear seemed unexpectedly. Nadia Russ never uses eraser. If a mistake made, it visually disappear when she draws new patterns. Her drawings are the pure improvisation with the ink pen.

NeoPopRealism ink pen/ pattern drawing concept

An artist draws a line that creates sections. Then, these sections filled with different repetitive patterns, some sections must be left blank. Eraser never used: if a mistake made, the continuing drawing of repetitive pattern balances the whole composition and make this mistake invisible. This is intuitive, imaginative, and meditative drawing. Using this concept, an artist can build the fascinating designs - simple or complicated - that can be used as the backgrounds for more realistic drawings. Also, artists can insert patterns into the realistic images. For example, eyebrows or lips spaces can be filled with repetitive patterns, or 3-d light or dark shadows, more. This type of drawing can be compared with Jazz with its syncopation and accents that appear in unpredictable order. However, the seemed chaotically created images look very harmonic, logical, and balanced. This type of drawing helps develop the sense of harmony and composition. When you are trying to fix the mistakes without eraser you are strengthening your hidden abilities and develop your artistic skills, such as feeling of composition and sense of harmony.

NeoPopRealism 10 Canons for Happier Life:

1. Be beautiful;
2. Be creative and productive; never stop studying and learning;
3. Be peace-loving, positive-minded;
4. Do not accept communist philosophy;

5. Be free-minded, do the best you can to move the world to peace and harmony;
6. Be family oriented, self-disciplined;
7. Be free spirited. Follow your dreams, if they are not destructive, but constructive;
8. Believe in the Higher Power; god is one, it is harmony and striving for perfection;
9. Be supportive to those who needs you, be generous;
10. Create your life as a great adventurous story.

Nadia Russ biography

Nadia Russ (aka Nadejda Maloletneva) was born into a former professional military officer's family in ex-USSR. As a child, she began studying art from famous masters of the past through art books and reproductions, which her mother Vera was collecting in their home in Konotop. Nadia daily heard about and saw the reproductions of works of Leonardo da Vinci, Michelangelo, Rafael, contemporary Russian artists such as Petrov-Vodkin.

In her 19, Nadia moved to Moscow. She began painting and drawing seriously in 1989. then, she created her unique ink pen/ pattern drawing concept. She was fascinated with effects of contrasting and flatness. A few months later, her first innovative ink pen drawings were exhibited in a group exhibition in famous Moscow's Manege, and later, in other Moscow's art galleries. In 1992, she successfully showed her work - acrylic paintings and ink pen drawings - in New York City.

In 1996-2000, Nadia resided in the Bahamas, where her acrylic work on canvas gained some very special brightness. There, she got her pseudonym to her original 'Nadejda Maloletneva', which was easier to pronounce - 'Nadia Russ'. In 2000-2001, in Xanadu hotel, she operated her Art Gallery Club 13.

In 2000, Nadia Russ moved to the United States, where she lives up until present. January 4, 2003, Nadia Russ created a word NeoPopRealism, and manifested it internationally. In 2004, she created the NeoPopRealism 10 canons for happier life.

Today, her artworks on canvas and ink pen drawings are in the private and public collections including MOYA - Museum of Young Art in Vienna (Austria), Ukrainian Museum in New York City (USA), Historical Museum of Fort Lauderdale (USA), Simferopol and Sumy Art Museums in Ukraine, Kinsey Institute of Indiana University (USA), WEAM - World Erotic Art Museum in Miami (USA), Schacknow Museum of Fine Arts (FL, USA), Lebedyn and Konotop Art Museums (Ukraine), D. Burliuk Foundation (Ukraine), and other.

In 2008-2010, Nadia Russ founded and juried Int'l NeoPopRealism Starz Art competitions. She authored a few art-related books such as "NeoPopRealism Starz: 21st Century ART" two volumes, "New Millennium ART", "Fort Lauderdale 100: A Must-Have Collector's Edition." She is the founder (in 2007) of the NeoPopRealism Journal & Wonderpedia, publications online, dedicated to arts, culture, books, news, celebrities and more. Nadia Russ lives in New York City and Florida.

A list of instructional How-To-Draw NeoPopRealism books

Each book contains the visual step-by-step instructions of a few drawing projects and history of NeoPopRealism, the artist Nadia Russ' biography and inspirational chapter, the unfinished NeoPopRealism ink & pen pattern images-templates for practicing and pages for creating repetitive patterns' gallery, 10 NeoPopRealism canons for happier life and more.

1. *How to Draw NeoPopRealism Ink Images: Basics*, ISBN: 978-0615515755 (for middle, high school, adults)

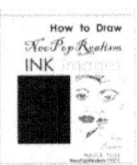

2. *How to Draw NeoPopRealism Abstract Images: Ink Backgrounds*, ISBN: 978-0615527437 (for middle, high school, adults)

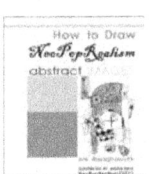

3. *How to Draw Advanced NeoPopRealism Ink Images*, ISBN: 978-0615569758 (for teens/ adults)

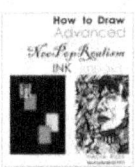

4. *How to Draw NeoPopRealism Abstract Images: Metallic Exuberance*, ISBN: 978-0615560991 (for teens/ adults)

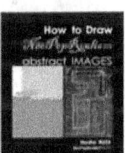

5. *How to Draw NeoPopRealism Color Abstract Images: Ink Backgrounds*, ISBN: 978-0615579559 (for teens/ adults)

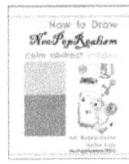

6. *How to Draw NeoPopRealism Advanced Abstract Images: Ink Backgrounds*, ISBN: 978-0615592558 (for teens/ adults)

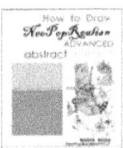

7. *How to Draw Without Eraser: Children's Guide to the World of NeoPopRealism*, ISBN: 978-0615521824 (for elementary)

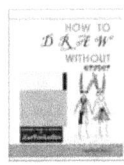

8. *How to Draw the NeoPopRealism Abstract: Children's Guide*, ISBN: 978-0615545332 (for elementary school)

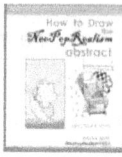

9. *NeoWhimsies: NeoPopRealism Ink Drawing Basics for Mannequins*, ISBN: 978-0615651859 (for children and craftsmen)

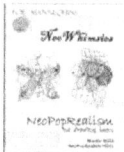

10. *NeoWhimsies for Beginners: 10 NeoPopRealism Ink Drawing Projects*, ISBN: 978-0615645087 (for elementary and middle school)

11. *First Steps: NeoWhimsies: NeoPopRealism Ink Drawing for Beginners*, ISBN: 978-0615641553 (for elementary and middle school)

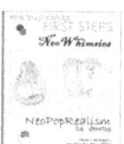

12. *Black Book for NeoPopRealism Metallic INK pen Drawing*, ISBN: 978-0615561028 (all ages sketchbook)

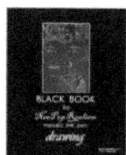

www.neopoprealism.org

www.ingramcontent.com/pod-product-compliance
Lightning Source LLC
Chambersburg PA
CBHW080934170526
45158CB00008B/2281

* 9 7 8 0 6 1 5 7 5 4 6 5 9 *